Dickson County, Tennessee

Marriages

1857—1870

Byron Sistler and Barbara Sistler

JANAWAY PUBLISHING, INC.
Santa Maria, California

Copyright © 1988 by Byron Sistler and Associates, Inc.

ALL RIGHTS RESERVED. Written permission must be secured from the
author or the publisher to use or reproduce any part of this book,
in any form or by any means, including electronic reproduction,
except for brief quotations in critical reviews or articles.

Originally Published:
Nashville, Tennessee
1988

Reprinted for
Byron Sistler and Associates, Inc.

by

Janaway Publishing, Inc.
732 Kelsey Ct.
Santa Maria, California 93454
(805) 925-1038
www.JanawayGenealogy.com

2006, 2013

ISBN: 978-1-59641-047-3

Made in the United States of America

DICKSON COUNTY, TN MARRIAGES
1857-1870

Where two dates appear on an entry, the first one is the date license was issued, the second (in parentheses) the date marriage was solemnized. If only one date, it usually means that the date of execution was the same as the date of license issuance.

Sometimes the execution of the marriage was not reported to the courthouse, and occasionally the clerk failed to note in the marriage book that the license was returned. We would usually make a notation in the entry to indicate the non-execution of a marriage if the book so stated.

The marriages are arranged alphabetically, the first half of the book by groom--the second by bride.

The records included in this book were transcribed by us directly from microfilmm of the original marriage books. Error, where it occurs, may be attributed to us, or to the clerks of the period, many of whom did an appallingly sloppy job of entering the information.

If the bride and groom were black, a B is placed at the end of the entry.

It should be remembered that this and other marriage books we have prepared are indexes, and do not include all the information to be found in the original marriage book. Such data as names of bondsmen, ministers, justices of the peace, churches, etc., are omitted. Often such information is helpful to the researcher. Consequently the serious researcher, to obtain this additional information as well as to check on the accuracy of the transcriber, should examine the original marriage record if at all possible.

                                            Byron Sistler
                                            Barbara Sistler

                                            Nashville, TN
                                            January 1988

Abercrombie, A. to Rebecca J. Adams 1-11-1866
Adams, Ancel to Sarah Jane Mathis 5-19-1857 (5-19-1857)
Adams, Benjamin S. to Mary E. Waynick 12-14-1866
Adams, Edward to Bettie Sinks 1-24-1864
Adams, James to Elizabeth Jane Heath 11-26-1866
Adams, James to Kanzadie Gilland 3-21-1866 (3-22-1866)
Adams, Jiles to Catherine Bond 4-2-1866
Adams, John to Mary A. Adams 9-13-1858 (9-14-1858)
Adams, John C. to Mary E. Waynick 6-10-1860
Adams, John I. J. to Nancy Moore 3-11-1858
Adams, P. H. to Betsey J. Mathis 1-24-1862
Adams, S. to E. Williams 11-27-1862
Adams, Stephen to Mary L. Mathis 8-27-1868 (8-31-1868)
Adams, W. J. to Anna E. May 2-26-1866 (2-27-1866)
Adams, W. M. to Tennessee D. Daniel 1-11-1866 (1-15-1866)
Adams, W. W. to Frances Turner 9-25-1864
Adcock, G. to N. J. Murrell 6-3-1864 (6-5-1864)
Adcock, George to M. C. McCoy 5-26-1870
Adcock, J. B. to Sarah Richardson 8-23-1865 (8-24-1865)
Adcock, J. W. to Missouri Fussell 1-31-1867
Adcock, Jesse H. to Lucindy A. Adcock 1-?-1868
Adcock, M. V. to Susan Cathey no date (with Oct 1866)
Adcock, M. V. to Susan Cathy 10-25-1866 (10-28-1866)
Adcock, S. H. to R. E. Myatt 10-22-1870 (10-27-1870)
Adkins, Saml. H. to E. F. Swift 9-2-1864 (9-15-1864)
Akin, Thomas J. to Sarah Cook 10-4-1865
Albright, John to Sophronia Reynolds 10-16-1858 (10-17-1858)
Allbrooks, F. M. to Mary J. Baker 3-14-1861
Allen, George S. to Jennette M. Oakley 3-18-1862
Allen, James M. to Juley G. McNeilley 10-6-1870
Allen, James N. to E. J. McNeely 4-23-1863
Allen, Samuel J.? to Sarah L. Cooksey 5-25-1867 (5-26-1867)
Allen, W. C. to Sarah A. Dickson 12-28-1866 (1-1-1867)
Allison, Hugh to Nannie Allison 2-13-1858 (2-16-1858)
Allison, Joseph to Jane Matthews 8-22-1868
Alsbrooks, George W. to Isabella Coleman 4-25-1870
Anchor, Allen to Agnes M. Turner 2-28-1870 (3-3-1870)
Anderson, Jas. to Nancy J. Gower 12-30-1862 (12-31-1862)
Anderson, Matt to Lucy Jane Larkins 12-23-1869
Anderson, Thos. J. to Clara E. Truby 5-15-1869 (5-18-1869)
Andrews, E. Y. to N. E. Myatt 9-30-1864
Anfienson, Thos. to America Wooddy 7-23-1864
Anglin, J. W. to Sophrona Tidwell 4-1-1859
Anglin, M. V. to Margaret Tidwell 8-27-1864
Anglin, T. J. to Artela Tate 1-17-1866
Austin, A. N. to Elizabeth Catharine Austin 12-4-1865 (12-5-1865)
Austin, H. G. to Eliza Carr 11-25-1857
Austin, James D. to Mary Gentry 3-25-1857
Austin, Wm. to Geo. Ann Willey 9-18-1858 (9-19-1858)
Averett, J. E. to S. E. A. Jones 10-16-1867
Averett, W. C. to M. M. Vanhook 6-17-1858 (6-18-1858)

Bagwell, Stephen to Martha Timmons 6-4-1863 (6-5-1863)
Baird, J. B. to C. Hay 1-2-1864 (1-3-1864)
Baker, Augustin to Rachael Murrell 1-11-1859 (1-12-1859)
Baker, Benj. F. to Laurentine Hudson 10-20-1866
Baker, Blount to L. C. Hutson 9-7-1860 (9-20-1860)
Baker, G. W. to E. J. Finch 12-26-1866 (1-2-1867)
Baker, George W. to Sarah Brown 7-18-1866 (7-21-1866)
Baker, John H. to Malvina Jackson 2-16-1870
Baker, Latham? G. to Martha C. Doty 12-20-1870
Baker, Nicholas to Arbella Murphy 11-16-1868
Baker, Tho. to Elvira Turner 11-7-1860
Baker, Wiley J. to Nancy E. Simmons 2-26-1868 (3-1-1868)
Baker, Wm. C. to Sallie M. Allbright 10-12-1866 (10-14-1866)
Baldwin, R. M. to Hula B. Overton 8-9-1864 (8-10-1864)
Ballard, Richard H. to Jennetta Ragan 8-24-1857 (9-1-1857)
Balthrop, Mackallen to Bettey Ann Craigh 10-30-1869 (10-31-1869)
Bateman, Henry A. to Parthena F. Deen 3-28-1866
Bateman, Isaac to Martha Ann Austin 7-2-1870
Bateman, W. J. W. to Elanora Story 4-14-1864
Bateman, Wiley H. to Mary Steeley 6-15-1870 (6-16-1870)
Batson, W. B. to Lydia J. Sensing 10-6-1857 (10-8-1857)
Beard, Jacob to Almarinda Sellers 11-12-1864 (11-16-1864)
Beasley, William to Allice Elliott 5-28-1866 (5-29-1866)
Beck, John T. to M. G. Shelton 11-2-1858 (11-3-1858)
Bell, A. H. to E. C. Stuart 4-2-1862 (4-9-1862)
Bellfield, Lawrence to Amanda Jackson 12-25-1866 (12-28-1866)
Bensinger, Wm. to Sarah Harris 2-2-1864 (2-11-1864)
Berry, W. J. W. J. to Amanda Hudson 11-20-1869 (11-21-1869)
Berry, W. N. M. to N. A. W. Nesbitt 11-26-1864 (12-6-1864)
Binkley, W. H. to Ann J. Mathews 1-6-1862 (1-9-1862)
Bird, Chas. to Polly Ann Murrell 10-20-1862 (10-22-1862)
Bishop, Asa to Sophronia Shadic 4-8-1864 (4-10-1864)
Bishop, J. H. to Sallie Miller 5-25-1867 (5-26-1867)
Black, John to Nancy Bishop 7-8-1864
Black, Michael to Mary A. Christie 10-6-1858 (10-7-1858)
Blackburn, John to Malona Dunnagan 2-15-1858 (2-23-1858)
Blackwell, Thomas to Mary E. Simmons 8-23-1868
Bledsoe, William T. to Nancy E. Williams 3-26-1868
Blocker, T. P. to I. J. Nicks 1-19-1867 (1-20-1867)
Blount, Thos. J. to Frank? E. Deen 5-16-1861
Boaz, Joel N. to Susan A. Dillehay 2-4-1859
Boaze, J. D. to M. E. Russell 8-18-1864 (8-25-1864)
Bond, L. S. to M. C. Lamastus 2-29-1864
Bone, A. H. to D. A. Foster 1-15-1867
Bone, A. H. to H. F. Bledsow 11-18-1864 (11-20-1864)
Bone, Geo. K. to Martha J. Slayden 1-19-1864 (1-20-1864)
Bone, Thos. T. to Margaret L. T. Cagle 1-13-1859
Bone, William B. to R. E. Slayden 10-8-1870 (10-11-1870)
Booker, Jas. to Amanda Davidson 12-27-1864 (12-28-1864)
Booker, Robert to Susan A. Bowen 11-20-1858 (11-21-1858)
Booker, Thomas to Letty Tingler 5-2-1870 (5-8-1870)
Bowen, E. L. to Maranda Whitlock 1-9-1864 (1-10-1864)

Bowers, J. M. to M. C. Cayce 11-1-1865 (11-13-1865)
Bowker (Booker?), James M. to Sarah E. Bishop 5-14-1870 (5-15-1870)
Bradford, Lee to Ann Waynick 10-22-1870
Bradford, Riley to Martha Underwood 8-11-1860 (8-12-1860)
Bradley, Charles A. to Mary A. Stuart 5-24-1860 (5-26-1860)
Brazel, J. M. to Sarah Springger 8-27-1866 (8-28-1866)
Brazzell, George to Louisa E. Dunnagan 1-20-1866 (1-21-1866)
Brazzell, James to Susan Goodrich 10-31-1863 (10-7?-1863)
Brazzell, James R. to Mary E. Martin 7-17-1858 (7-18-1858)
Brazzell, James R. to Sallie A. Martin 1-18-1869 (1-19-1869)
Brazzle, Henderson to Jane Tatom 12-28-1867 (12-29-1867)
Brewer, Ellas to L. E. Waynick 6-25-1870 (6-26-1870)
Briant, Ben F. to Fredonia A. Runnells? 12-26-1860
Briant, J. M. to Tennessee Baldwin 12-24-1869
Briant, John H. to Nancy J. Baldwin 12-27-1860
Brim, John to Susan V. Thompson 8-30-1870 (9-1-1870)
Brim, W. B. to Mary A. Perkins 7-8-1865 (7-9?-1865)
Brock, John to L. Hainy 2-14-1857 (2-15-1857)
Brown, A. P. to Mary Sutherland 10-27-1869
Brown, B. F. to Louisiana Garton 9-19-1862 (9-20-1862)
Brown, J. K. to Ann Greer 12-29-1857
Brown, Jackson to Rebecca Ladd 12-12-1860
Brown, James H. to Martha Ann Adams 8-16-1867 (8-17-1867)
Brown, James M. to Mary J. Stuart 12-24-1866 (12-7?-1866)
Brown, John to Mary Ladd 7-21-1865 (7-23-1865)
Brown, John to Nancy Lampley 2-2-1864 (2-7-1864)
Brown, Monroe to Elenory Ayers 5-28-1870
Brown, R. B. to J. M. Matlock 6-6-1865
Brown, W. M. to A. A. Southerland 12-22-1860 (12-23-1860)
Brown, W. S. to R. J. Vineyard 4-1-1861 (4-14-1861)
Brown, Wm. H. to Margaret A. Martin 11-19-1866
Browning, A. B. to M. P. Bailey 12-29-1865 (12-30-1865)
Bruce, Beverly to Levica Craft 7-7-1858 (7-13-1858)
Bruce, Dennis to Catherine Leathers 10-5-1863 (10-8-1863)
Bruce, James to C. Myatt 12-3-1863 (12-9-1863)
Bruce, Jno. M. to Elizabeth Frost 3-20-1860 (3-21-1860)
Bruce, Silas to Kisiah Leathers 9-22-1857
Brumit, William to Martha Hunter 9-30-1870
Bryant, D. J. to N. E. Bryant 1-22-1863
Bryant, James M. to Susan Haskins 9-11-1870
Bryant, Wm. to E. A. Henley 4-3-1860 (4-4-1860)
Bryles, Hiram to E. R. Howell 7-28-1862
Bull, J. B. to Dilly Ann Taylor 3-2-1866 (3-8-1866)
Bullard, Danl. to Elizabeth Warner 2-19-1862 (2-20-1862)
Burn, Thomas W. to Missouri Baker 12-27-1868
Burrows?, John H. to Ellen A. Jones 1-19-1864 (1-24-1864)
Bush, Wm. to R. C. Cooley 8-7-1864 (8-8-1864)
Butler, Aaron B. to Tennessee A. Petty 12-26-1867 (12-22?-1867)
Buttery, Wm. to Eliza White 1-26-1857 (1-2?-1857)
Buttrey, James to Tennessee Lampley 11-26-1868 (12-17-1868)
Buttrey, W. G. L. to Louisa E. Anglin 7-27-1866 (7-31-1866)
Byars, John to Rebecca Price 8-8-1864 (8-9-1864)

Bybee, James L. to Araminnta M. James 9-8-1866
Byers, John to Evaline Rose 2-16-1859
Byres, J. B. to Rebecca F. Coon 1-25-1860 (1-29-1860)
Caldwell, O. D. to Nancy J. Long 1-5-1867 (1-6-1867)
Callen, Henry C. to E. C. Woodward 8-25-1857
Campbell, David A. to Amandey Hambrick 1-12-1863
Campbell, R. M. to V. L. M. Hibbs 5-30-1864 (5-31-1864)
Capeheart, F. to W. A. Thompson 5-17-1864 (5-19-1864)
Capps, Alfred S. to Adeline E. Thompson 9-8-1862 (9-10-1862)
Capps, E. E. to Susan Kellum 7-29-1863
Capps, Wilson to Allice P. Jones 11-9-1865
Carr, Alex to Mary J. Carr 8-3-1864 (8-5-1864)
Carr, Thomas J. to Tennessee C. Porter 12-24-1867 (12-26-1867)
Carrall, C. M. to E. V. Proctor 2-2-1862 (2-3-1862)
Carrall, Wm. to Susan Williams 8-15-1861
Carrell, James A. to Martha A. Briant 9-11-1869 (9-12-1869)
Carroll, R. M. to Sarah E. Cunningham 2-6-1858 (2-7-1858)
Carroll, W. W. to M. E. Cunningham 8-10-1864
Carter, W. G. to Ludeena Thompson 6-17-1857
Caselman, John to Lathersy? Spencer 1-12-1867 (1-13-1867)
Cathey, Archabald to Susan E. Brown 2-1-1860
Cathey, E. N. to Lucindy M. Brown 2-10-1866 (2-11-1866)
Cathey, F. M. to Elizabeth Tate 1-16-1861 (1-17-1861)
Cathey, Joshua to Mary A. Hood 6-23-1857 (6-24-1857)
Cathey, Morris R. to M. A. F. Lewallen 8-23-1859 (8-24-1859)
Cathey, S. W. to Sarah Davidson 4-22-1864 (5-5-1864)
Cathey, S. W. to Sarah A. Davidson 12-28-1865
Caufman, John to Elizabeth Joslin 2-?-1858 (2-10-1858)
Chadoin, R. to Elizabeth Jones 12-1-1860 (12-3-1860)
Chadwick, Jacob to Martha A. Dunnagan 12-21-1867 (12-22-1867)
Chapel, Jas. to Nancy Climer 4-14-1865 (4-30-1865)
Chappell, W. D. to R. Jane Gossett (Garrett?) 3-29-1858 (4-1-1858)
Charuthers, John to Lucinda Garland 4-18-1870 (4-19-1870)
Chesman, Jacob to Susan A. E. Vanhook 3-13-1858 (3-14-1858)
Chester, T. B. to Mary E. Ragen 1-11-1869
Chilton, J. L. to S. E. Baker 1-19-1864
Chilton, J.? L. to Sarah E. Baker 8-19?-1865
Choat, J. F. to M. D. England 10-23-1869 (10-24-1869)
Choat, James to Mary Duke 12-17-1870 (12-18-1870)
Choat, Joseph to Mary J. England 12-22-1868
Choat, S. E. to Frances Williams 12-20-1866
Clancy, Martin to Mary J. Marsh? 9-28-1860 (9-29-1860)
Clardy, George to Anna Walker 11-20-1865 (11-21-1865)
Clark, Benj. G. to Mary J. Nesbitt 1-21-1858
Clifton, J. K. to Tennesse ann Dudley 7-31-1865 (8-3-1865)
Clifton, M. W. to Mahala Tidwell 10-26-1859 (10-27-1859)
Climer, Charley to Margaret Underwood 3-10-1858
Climer, F. M. to S. F. Crane 8-28-1857
Cloud, J. F. to Malinda Oliver 10-21-1863
Cloud?, M. R. to R. V. Ward 10-6-1860
Clymer?, Wm. to Jane C. Underwood 2-21-1861 (2-23-1861)
Coalman, Samuel to Jack Ann Glasgow 2-23-1870 (2-24-1870)

Collin, Jno. M. to Mary E. Shelton 1-1-1859 (1-2-1859)
Collins, W. T. to S. M. Littrel 3-4-1859 (3-10-1859)
Colter, C. N. to S. E. Sitton 5-5-1864
Conklin, J. F. to Bettie Bowen 4-29-1868
Cook, Austin to Sarah Chambers 4-30-1858
Cooley, E. C. to Mary A. Lewis 7-8-1858 (7-10-1858)
Cooley, L. B. to Lucy A. Matlock 9-26-1867
Cooley, M. to F. C. Jones 8-22-1864
Copley, J. H. to E. G. Pamenter? 12-28-1870
Cording, J. B. to R. J. Pavatt 5-11-1859
Corey, George to E. R. Pickett 7-27-1870 (7-30-1870)
Corlew, Henderson to Mary A. Hughes 12-21-1859 (12-22-1859)
Corlew, James M. to Mary T. Pavatt 10-5-1870
Cowen, Wm. to Nancy Guinn 4-14-1858 (4-15-1858)
Cox, S. W. to Mary W. Rains 12-18-1860 (12-20-1860)
Coyne, John to Mary M. Lawson 3-29-1860 (6-18-1860)
Craft, L. M. to A. J. Dunnagan 8-12-1863
Craig, J. E. to Martha A. Adkins 9-2-1868 (9-3-1868)
Craig, W. J. to Sarah L. (C.?) James 3-12-1858 (3-14-1858)
Craige, R. F. M. to R. A. Parrish 11-2-1864 (11-3-1864)
Craigh, J. B. to Harriett B. Ray 7-15-1868
Creach, John to Frances Linzey 3-7-1870 (3-8-1870)
Creasey, Jordan W. to Levana Bull 12-22-1863 (12-24-1863)
Creech, Benj. to Nelly Joslin 11-23-1864 (11-27-1864)
Crim, James H. to Mary E. Washburn 12-14-1868 (12-15-1868)
Critchard, J. C. R. to Mary Matlock 12-12-1863
Crow, M. R. to Polly A. Adcock 12-6-1858 (12-7-1858)
Crow, S. M. to Eliza Heath 7-12-1870
Crowell, Wm. S. to Matilda J. Walker 1-26-1859 (1-27-1859)
Crown, A. J. H. to Bettie N. Hartigan 8-31-1859 (9-1-1859)
Crunk, W. C. to E. E. Shelton 7-23-1869
Cullum, Jesse P. to Martha T. Cullum 5-1-1869 (5-3-1869)
Cunningham, B. W. to Malissa A. Gordon 7-7-1857 (7-12-1857)
Cunningham, John F. to Eliza J. Tidwell 9-18-1865 (9-19-1865)
Curtis, Eli T. to Mary A. Dunnagan 9-12-1857 9-13-1857)
Damell, L. W. to L. W. Shelton 9-18-1863
Daniel, Geo. W. to M. A. Loggins 12-12-1864 (12-29-1864)
Daniel, J. C. to Mary Loggins 10-7-1857
Daniel, J. S. to R. A. Larkins 7-28-1864
Daniel, Jos. to Mary P. Daniel 11-18-1861
Daniel, Richard to Tabitha Spicer 12-26-1867
Daniel, W. R. to Rebecca Pendergrass 8-3-1858 (8-4-1858)
Daugherty, J. W. to Elizabeth Howell 5-24-1858 (5-27-1858)
Daughterty, John to M. E. Chapel 4-14-1865
Daverson, Elijah to Rachael M. Crow 2-21-1867
Davidson, Thomas M. to Margaret Cathey 7-14-1866 (7-15-1866)
Davidson, William to Laura N. Ferrell 4-6-1869 (4-7-1869
Davidson, William to Mary V. Hughes 12-25-1866
Davidson, Wm. to Nancy W. Shelton 12-23-1857 (12-24-1857)
Davis, Henry to Meshia McCrary 6-2-1868 (6-7-1868)
Davis, Houston to E. E. Spradlin 4-2-1859
Davis, J. F. to Eliza A. Harvey 12-31-1869 (1-5-1870)

Dawson, E. J. to N. M. Walker 12-23-1869
Deal, George P. to Mary A. Jones 7-28-1866 (7-30-1866)
Dean, W. C. to E. E. Stokes 11-24-1859
Deason, Philip H. to Martha Mathis 9-14-1865
Deason, Wm. R. to L. T. Stoke 8-27-1864
Decker, G. M. to Geo. Ann Hill 3-10-1858
Deen, J. W. to Polly W. Sensing 5-2-1861
Deen, Wiley B. to S. M. Walker 9-22-1870
Deloch, Gilbert to Martha J. Price 10-12-1870
Denny, Henry to M. A. Goodin 6-6-1864
Derryberry, John H. to Louvina Reep 12-20-1869 (1-20-1870)
Dickson, Geo. M. to M. A. Gillmore 10-17-1864 (10-20-1864)
Dickson, Thos. L. T. to Sarah Browning 7-22-1858 (7-25-1858)
Dickson, Wm. H. to P. D. Dickson 12-27-1866
Dickson, Wm. J. to Mary M. Robertson 10-11-1859
Dillard, Franklin to Mary Jane Grove 3-31-1866 (4-1-1866)
Dilyard, John to Huldy Garton 1-4-1866 (1-3?-1866)
Dobson, J. B. to Fannie Gadby 3-25-1861
Dodson, J. B. to Mary Reaves 1-7-1860 (1-8-1860)
Dorrin (Dunn?), W. M. to Narcissy R. Sutherland 3-31-1870
Dotson, J. C. to Araminta Jackson 2-3-1858
Dotson, J. W. to Nancy C. Streat 6-30-1858 (7-1-1858)
Dotson, S.? M. to Cora Cooksey 6-25-1867 (6-27-1867)
Doty, John A. to Mary E. Baker 12-20-1870 (12-21-1870)
Dudley, Anthony F. to Clara Loftis 12-7-1859 (12-8-1859)
Duke, H. L. to L. A. McCormick 7-9-1870 (7-10-1870)
Duke, Robert A. to Martha A. Johnson 10-8-1859 (10-13-1859)
Duncan, Wm. to Frances Hibbs 2-12-1864
Dunlap, John A. to Mary C. Larkins 1-3-1865
Dunnagan, A. C. to Adline Few 2-6-1867
Dunnagan, Abner to Rachel Tidwell 2-28-1865
Dunnagan, J. C. to Mary S. Adcock 1-10-1869
Dunnagan, James R. to F. C. Brown 10-23-1858 (10-24-1858)
Dunnagan, John C. to Amanda L. Dudley 3-4-1868 (3-5-1868)
Dunnagan, Madison to Sarah Miller 5-14-1870 (5-15-1870)
Dunnagan, W. F. to E. Phillipps 7-7-1859 (7-21-1859)
Easley, John W. to Elizabeth Sugg 3-12-1857
Edney, W. N. to E. A. Frasher 3-22-1861 (3-24-1861)
Edwards, James to Rebecca Ann Dodson 12-1-1869 (12-2-1869)
Edwards, Joseph to Dealatha J. Hall 2-18-1868 (2-20-1868)
Eleazer, W. D. to Dolly H. Dodson 1-30-1867
Elliott, S. M. to M. E. Finch 4-8-1865 (4-10-1865)
Elliott, Stokley to Mary E. Nance 4-7-1866 (4-8-1866)
England, James J. to Nancy C. Harrell 12-22-1860 (12-24-1860)
England, James S. to Susan Dodson 2-5-1869 (2-6-1869)
England, R. G. to M. C. Baker 12-20-1866
England, R. L. to Geo. Ann Martin 9-18-1858 (9-19-1858)
England, Thomas to Mary Evans 3-2-1867
England, W. W. to N. M. Nash 2-4-1867 (2-8-1867)
Epps, G. P. Y. to Martha E. Hall 3-14-1866
Erington, Joel jr. to M. L. Few 12-25-1866 (12-30-1866)
Erlinger, Levi W. to Mattie D. Pickett 3-4-1867

Errington, Joel to Sarah Bryant 10-28-1867 (11-29-1867)
Estes, George J. to Anna Richardson 1-6-1869
Estes, Joshua G. to Elizer Thomas 8-31-1868 (9-3-1868)
Etheridge, Geo. to Mary Dugger 5-20-1857 (5-21-1857)
Etheridge, Wm. to Elizabeth Goodwin 7-18-1860
Eubank, Richd. D. to Lucinda Corlew 12-18-1860
Evans, Frank to Margaret Heath 5-9-1864
Evans, G. W. to Matilda Few 11-12-1862 (11-20-1862)
Evans, Saml. H. to Sarah J. Wilkins 9-13-1858 (9-14-1858)
Farhan, John to Mary M. Tidwell 8-5-1861 (8-8-1861)
Felts, J. L. to Polly Hatley 3-18-1861 (3-19-1861)
Fentress, Jas. J. to Victoria S. Stanfill 4-29-1865
Fielder, J. M. to L. D. Smith 7-27-1870
Finney, C. to M. J. Terrel 6-7-1864 (6-9-1864)
Finnie?, James to L. J. Foster 10-17-1862 (10-19-1862)
Fisher, Martin to Mary Owens 7-22-1864 (7-23-1864)
Fletcher, George to Martha Ellen Fowlkes 6-4-1870 (6-5-1870)
Fletcher, R. E. to Eliza Jane Smith 9-13-1859 (9-14-1859)
Folay, Thos. to Mary Conaly 9-24-1860
Ford, Jesse M. to Sarah Anderson 3-6-1866
Ford, William J. to Rebecca A. Sensing 10-22-1866 (10-23-1866)
Forsythe, Jerry to Mary E. Sensing 9-20-1866 (9-30-1866)
Forsythe, John to Martha E. Sensing 7-4-1867
Foster, J. F. to S. A. Carroll 18-6-1857
Foster, James W. to Martha J. Parrott 12-23-1859 (12-27-1859)
Foster, John Frank to Tabitha J. Self 12-17-1858
Fowler, James to Mary Jane Fowler 9-9-1865 (9-10-1865)
Fowler, M. T. to Susan Owens 7-28-1870 (7-31-1870)
Franklin, Louis M. to Sarah Murrell 8-24-1865
Frasher, James R. to Lucinda P. Austin 2-11-1858
Frasher, Pleasant to Sarah E. Frasher 8-17-1866 (8-19-1866)
Frasher, W. P. A. to Rebecca H. Parker 6-20-1862
Freeman, P. C. to Mary E. Weakley 4-15-1863 (4-16-1863)
Freeman, Tho. M. W. to M. J. Cunningham 5-29-1861 (5-30-1861)
Fry, Levi G. to Mallinda Johnson 10-12-1869 (11-10-1869)
Fulks, H. W. to Martha T. Godwin 2-25-1870 (2-21?-1870)
Furgerson, J. F. to Margarett C. Baker 12-29-1869
Gafford, J. M. to Louisa Linzey 5-2-1868
Gafford, J. P. to Missouria Linzey 7-10-1866 (7-13-1866)
Gafford, W. J. to Nancy D. Kephart 12-27-1865
Garland, Orvel to Catharine Varden 1-7-1867
Garland, S. J. to S. B. Sims? 6-23-1865 (6-25-1865)
Garton, Griffith to Bettie Brown 4-17-1869
Gentry, David G. to Ferby Meek 1-5-1867 (1-6-1867)
Gentry, H. C. to Lenora Richardson 5-14-1870 (5-25-1870)
Gentry, James L. to Lucinda P. Petty 5-15-1869 (5-16-1869)
Gentry, James P. to Fredonia Harris 3-21-1866
Gentry, M. L. to Amanda Tidwell 4-23-1870 (4-24-1870)
Gentry, Mathew L. to Mary J. Harris 1-9-1860 (1-10-1860)
Gentry, Thos. B. to Comfort Meek 12-5-1863 (not executed)
Geurin (Guinn?), A. V. to E. F. Slayden 12-26-1865 (12-28-1865)
Giddings, E. W. to Hetty E. Ayers 5-11-1870 (5-19-1870)

Gilbert, James M. to Myrom? Toler 11-25-1867
Gill, J. W. to Louisa C. Joslin 8-8-1865 (8-10-1865)
Gilleland, James C. to Ellen Price 1-23-1867
Gillmore, R. M. to Letticia Taylor 4-29-1864
Gilmore, Saml. F. to Jaldean? Mitchell 11-19-1857 (11-20-1857)
Glasgow, C. M. to Jack Ann Hunter 10-15-1862 (10-16-1862)
Glasgow, J. M. to Mary F. Hunter 12-3-1869 (12-5-1869)
Glass, James to Jemima Pendergrass 8-6-1860
Glassgo, J. M. to Martha G. Hunter 10-21-1858
Godfry, J. W. to M. J. Rice 11-11-1863 (11-12-1863)
Goforth, William M. to A. C. L. Reed 6-25-1867 (6-27-1867)
Goodlet, A. G. jr. to Florance Gold 6-8-1866 (6-10-1866)
Goodrich, B. F. to Frances Butler? 8-7-1858 (8-12-1858)
Goodrich, Benjamin to Tennessee Pettey 2-29-1868 (3-1-1868)
Goodrich, E. B. to Emily Sanders 11-5-1869 (11-14-1869)
Goodwin, R. to Martha A. Adcock 2-24-1859
Goostree, Rufus J. to Rachael A. Henton 9-7-1868 (9-8-1868)
Gray, James W. to Sarah R. P. Barns 7-25-1860 (7-26-1860)
Green, James W. to Aneliza E. Coleman 1-17-1870 (1-25-1870)
Green, Joseph M. to Nancy M. Hopper 8-11-1865
Green, W. H. to Susan Dunnagan 2-9-1870
Green, W. M. to H. P. Thornton? 11-30-1858 (12-1-1858)
Green, Wm. M. to H. C. Tomlinson 8-9-1864 (8-11-1864)
Griffin, A. S. to M. A. Lampley 2-28-1865 (3-1-1865)
Griffin, Wm. to Sallie Cunningham 10-20-1863
Grove, G. L. to Tennessee A. Ladd 10-10-1867
Grove, Jno. T. to Elizabeth D. Edwards 4-7-1862
Groves, Z. M. to Martha Ann Phillips 12-28-1869
Grymes, James B. to Margaret Phipps 1-21-1863 (1-22-1863)
Grymes, John B. to Nancy A. Dodson 11-11-1858
Guinn, William H. to Sarah E. Gray 2-18-1868 (2-19-1868)
Gunn, A. J. to Louisa D. Crawford 12-27-1868 (12-31-1868)
Gunn, Henry C. to Elizabeth A. Nesbitt 12-1-1866 (12-2-1866)
Gunn, John R. to Mary A. Hedge 1-3-1861 (1-6-1861)
Gunn?, T. D. to Frances Rogers 2-2-1859 (2-3-1859)
Hagey, W. J. to J. E. Martin 9-24-1870 (9-25-1870)
Hagwood, William to Mary E. Jackson 3-28-1867
Hale, Thos. M. to Nannie? A. McLaughlin 11-1-1859 (11-30-1859)
Haley, H. W. to Mary E. Baker 10-28-1861 (11-7-1861)
Haley, James to Nancy Haley 3-13-1860 (3-15-1860)
Hall, Ben F. to Mary Brown 3-19-1862 (3-20-1862)
Hall, J. H. to Emiline Lampley 12-18-1864 (12-19-1864)
Hall, J. M. to Susan Carr 3-10-1858
Hall, Joseph to Sarah Taylor 10-12-1860 (10-14-1860)
Hall, Thomas E. to Mary Perry 7-18-1867 (7-21-1867)
Hall, William C. to Sarah Luther 1-13-1870
Hallaburton, George to Rody A. Willey 2-13-1866
Halliburton, Chas. to Mencacy? Browning 12-25-1860 (1-13-1861)
Halliburton, M. A. to L. F. Climer 10-3-1857 (10-5-1857)
Halliburton, Tho. to R. J. Bower 8-15-1857 (8-16-1857)
Halliburton, Turner to Virginia A. Booze 11-7-1866 (11-8-1866)
Hamilton, P. H. to Jane Rail 5-29-1865

Hamilton, Robert to Martha Gray 9-30-1865 (10-1-1865)
Hammon, Samuel to Clary E. Herberson 9-24-1866 (10-17-1866)
Hammond, Jno. to Rena Byler 8-28-1863
Hampton, John A. to Mary E. Link 2-21-1868 (2-28-1868)
Hampton, Martin to Malvina Ferrel 12-7-1866 (12-9-1866)
Handlin, Tho. J. to Mary S. Street? 5-21-1859 (5-22-1859)
Haney, John? to H.? M.? Gray 9-15-1870
Hargroves, T. to E. West 7-25-1859
Harley, W. H. to Susan J. James 1-24-1857 (1-25-1857)
Harper, E. C. to A. G. Nicks 9-22-1870
Harris, E. J. to S. F. Corlew 3-5-1857
Harris, H. H. to H. T. Watley 4-11-1861
Harris, J. C. to Nannie F. Harris 12-18-1865 (12-21-1865)
Harris, N. B. to S. E. Edwards 1-2-1865 (1-3-1865)
Harris, Thomas B. to A. J. Linzey 8-2-1869 (8-3-1869)
Harris, Thos. J. to Martha Ann Richardson 12-31-1868
Harvey, Blount to Mary J. Morgan 1-12-1863 (1-15-1863)
Harvey, Jack to S. L. Hickerson 4-3-1858 (4-4-1858)
Harvey, Jas. to E. A. Bull 6-3-1864 (6-20-1864)
Harvey, Oney S. to Mary F. Hickerson 6-16-1866 (6-24-1866)
Harvy, J. T. to Rebecca A. Freeman 1-5-1867 (1-14-1867)
Hase, C. L. to Margarett Thomison 12-11-1865
Hase, Jas. to Sarah Legget 9-1-1864 (9-4-1864)
Hassel, George W. to Isabel Baker 5-26-1869 (5-30-1869)
Hassell, E. T. to Lucinda E. Potter 10-22-1859 (10-23-1859)
Hassell, James H. to Eliza J. Allbright 5-10-1870 (5-18-1870)
Hassell, W. B. to E. A. Finch 9-18-1861 (1-26-1862)
Hassum, Jos. to E. Welch 12-24-1861 (12-25-1861)
Hatcher, J. L. to Mary A. Sizemore 2-9-1857 (2-12-1857)
Hatcher, W. C. to Nancy E. Brazzell 2-1-1870 (2-3-1870)
Hatley, Gustin to Latitia Bella Thompson 1-10-1869
Hatley, Manley to Susan Mayfield 2-3-1859
Hatley, Manuel to J. E. Rose 10-25-1865 (10-29-1865)
Hay, Jno. M. to Mary E. Brown 3-15-1861 (3-17-1861)
Hays, McKenzy S. to Sarah M. Blackwell 1-27-1870
Hays, W. J. to Sarah Curtis 12-28-1861 (12-29-1861)
Hayse, J. R. B. to Mattilda J. Harley 12-26-1868 (12-27-1868)
Hayse, James to Mary Brown 1-16-1869 (1-17-1869)
Heard, James H. to E. J. Burger 10-30-1858 (10-31-1858)
Heath, E. to Susan Jackson 11-13-1861
Heath, Leroy to E. J. Tolar 3-20-1860 (3-21-1860)
Hedge, Jas. P. to M. J. Holland 12-22-1864
Henderson, H. H. to Elizer Dawson 2-7-1866
Henderson, John J. to C. L. Dunnaway 6-14-1859
Hendrick, J. A. to M. J. Larkins 7-31-1870
Hendrick, James to Arbella J. Michel 11-4-1867
Hendrick, Joseph H. to Sarah A. Thompson 12-31-1859
Hendrix, Will to Laury Bramlet 12-3-1869 (12-5-1869)
Henley, A. C. to E. E. Williams 4-5-1862 (4-6-1862)
Henley, Alfred C. to Susan Ann Carney 12-26-1868 (12-27-1868)
Henry, J. B. to R. L. Brown 5-3-1869 (5-6-1869)
Henson, J. B. to S. H. Jarnagan 9-11-1867

Herbison, R. B. to R. J. Prichard 8-18-1863
Hickerson, C. to A. F. Williams 8-18-1866 (8-19-1866)
Hickerson, D. R. to Martha A. Harvey 8-14-1858 (8-15-1858)
Higgins, J. J. to S. C. Manley 5-11-1868
Higgins, W. E. to M. A. Stringfellow 8-12-1870 (8-14-1870)
Hiland, M. M. to Louisa J. Jackson 11-26-1869
Hill, Geo. W. to P. E. Hall 9-3-1861
Hill, J. D. to N. J. Smith 8-15-1863 (8-17-1863)
Hill, Wm. to Susan A. Porter 4-16-1862
Hinson, J. G. jr. to Susan S. Jarnigan 2-26-1862 (2-27-1862)
Hirt, W. M. to Rebecca Ann Wright 11-7-1866 (1-20-1867)
Hodge, Warner to Isabella Kain 12-22-1870 (12-23-1870)
Hodges, John H. to Sarah C. Harris 2-10-1859
Hogin, John to Mary Burn 7-4-1868 (7-5-1868)
Hogins, W. M. to Susan Tidwell 7-12-1866
Holley, John to Jennetta G. Ballard 1-2-1866 (1-7-1866)
Hood, John N. to E. C. Jackson 9-1-1857
Hood, John N. to Nancy Hall 1-2-1869 (1-3-1869)
Hooper, George R. to Susan Porter 2-18-1869
Hooper, Jesse to Panie? Speight 2-24-1862 (2-27-1862)
Hooper, John R. to Salena E. Nicks 8-21-1869 (8-22-1869)
Hooper, Lavell H. to Sarah M. Tally 9-22-1860 (9-23-1860)
Hooper, Simpson H. to Sarah J. Sutherland 1-1-1866
Hooper, Thos. J. to E. J. Wright 10-6-1860 (10-7-1860)
Hopper, Jacob to S. A. Dodson 9-15-1864
Horner, C. W. to Elizabeth Butler 4-6-1858
Howard, M. to Lucy E. Hanks 9-18-1857 (9-20-1857)
Hudgens, Wm. James to Emily McCall 1-12-1860
Hudson, D. F. to Susan E. Ennis 8-3-1863
Hudson, Dennis to Martha Southerland 9-7-1861 (9-8-1861)
Hudson, J. H. to A. J. Anglin 1-5-1866 (1-9-1866)
Hudson, John M. to Tennessee J. Walker 2-7-1865
Hudson, Robert A. to Sarah Elizabeth Bone 5-19-1866 (5-20-1866)
Huggeans, F. M. to Missourea F. Prockter 1-5-1867 (1-6-1867)
Huggins, John to Mary R. Nicks 3-7-1869
Hughes, James J. to Fredonia Kee 12-22-1870
Hughes, Wm. D. to Elizabeth Tucker 9-16-1870
Hughes, Wm. H. to Annette Dunn 5-31-1867
Hughs, John J. to Missouri J. Baldwin 10-7-1857
Hunt, James C. to S. P. Slayden 11-17-1858
Hunt, W. H. to M. A. Nichols 10-13-1863
Hunter, Albert to Elizabeth Cruise 2-5-1860
Hunter, Burrel to Letsy Slayden 3-28-1870
Hunter, J.W. to M. A.? Pinson 12-3-1863 (12-6-1863)
Hunter, James to Sarah E. Bull 6-24-1869
Hunter, Washington to Martha Joslin 6-15-1867
Hunter, William B. to Mary M. Pinson 5-22-1869 (5-23-1869)
Hutchison, William M. to Calledonia White 11-16-1868 (11-19-1868)
Hyde, Jackson to M. E. McCrary 8-18-1864 (8-22-1864)
Isbell, Thos. J. to E. L. Yeats 7-28-1870 (7-29-1870)
Jackson, Ben A. to Elizabeth Hatley 7-15-1858
Jackson, C. C. to D. A. Jackson 4-13-1863

Jackson, J. L. to M. P. Brazzel 5-31-1865 (6-1-1865)
Jackson, Jas. S. to Malita McMahan 3-14-1865
Jackson, John V. to Willella F. Mathis 11-12-1868
Jackson, Judge to Emily Mitchel 3-21-1870
Jackson, Parson to Sarah J. Garrett (Gossett?) 12-11-1867 (12-17-1867)
Jackson, R. P. to Nancy C. Stuart 6-30-1857 (7-1-1857)
Jackson, W. H. to Mahala T. Matlock 9-29-1865
James, John R. to Nancy Dawson 11-27-1865
James, Thomas J. to Nancy J. Hutson 11-21-1870 (11-24-1870)
Jarmon, James to Sallie Foster 6-30-1860 (7-1-1860)
Jarnagan, T. C. to Margaret R. Bowen 6-28-1869 (7-8-1869)
Jeans, Carter to Susan C. Nelson 1-10-1862 (1-13-1862)
Jenkins, J. T. to Nancy J. Chaudoin 1-19-1864 (1-20-1864)
Johnson, B. H. to M. H. Richardson 12-6-1864 (not certified)
Johnson, Britton to E. A. Hood 4-9-1859 (3-10-1859?)
Johnson, F. P. to M. A. Davidson 10-17-1864 (not certified)
Johnson, Henry N. to Sarah Ann Davidson 1-25-1866 (1-28-1866)
Johnson, R. A. to Elizabeth Davidson 9-3-1859 (9-4-1859)
Johnson, William to Susan C. James 12-23-1867 (12-24-1867)
Johnston, J. T. to Bedy E. Tidwell 1-27-1866 (1-28-1866)
Jones, Benjamin F. to Caroline Chadowin 7-22-1869 (7-26?-1869)
Jones, Edward T. to Florence Zodake 11-1-1870
Jones, Fountain to Elizabeth Taylor 8-9-1869 (8-11-1869)
Jones, Franklin to Agnes Herrin 5-6-1867 (5-9-1867)
Jones, J. G. to Fannie E. Bowen 12-28-1870
Jones, John A. to Mary A. Hall 1-30-1860 (2-8-1860)
Jones, W. J. to P. J. Bowen 8-16-1865 (8-17-1865)
Jordan, Ben to Susan Brown 1-2-1860 (1-3-1860)
Jordon, Montgomery to Martha J. Stokes 12-28-1867 (12-29-1867)
Joslin, W. B. to M. E. Whitfield 7-12-1864 (7-15-1864)
Joslin, W. B. to Mary J. Swinney 7-10-1869 (7-11-1869)
Justice, James E. to Ann J. Hiland 10-8-1859 (10-12-1859)
Justice, Thos. L. to Sarah J. Williams 5-29-1860 (5-31-1860)
Kain, William O. to Elizabeth Hegwood 12-24-1866 (12-26-1866)
Kamey, J. C. to Missouri Norris 9-30-1865 (10-8-1865)
Kapehart, C. M. to M. E. Owens 5-14-1870
Karns, Joseph to Louisa Brown 12-17-1864 (12-18-1864)
Kee, Wm. R. to Mary Bishop 8-5-1864
Kelly, J. C. R. to E. G. A. Chester 1-8-1869 (1-10-1869)
Keys, William to C. C. Hogan 7-19-1870 (7-21-1870)
Kiertner, C. H. to Emily Morgan 2-23-1857 (2-12?-1857)
King, Henderson to Martha Mitchel 9-1-1866 (9-2-1866)
Kinser, W. M. to Janie Fox 9-5-1870 (9-6-1870)
Kirk, Wm. M. to Sarah Hendrick 12-25-1860
Ladd, John O. to Agness McKechnie 2-13-1861 (2-14-1861)
Ladd, T. J. to Nelly Shelton 1-18-1870 (1-19-1870)
Ladd, W. H. to Mary A. Luther 9-30-1862
Laine, Alford to Elizabeth Long 10-17-1858
Lamastis, W. H. to Marry A. Brown 3-15-1866
Lamastus, Geo. to Eliza Jane Baker 8-12-1857 (8-13-1857)
Lampley, Andrew J. to Mary E. Bishop 7-4-1862 (7-13-1862)
Lampley, J. W. to Louisa Phillips 12-27-1864 (12-31-1864)

Lampley, William G. to Sarena C. Sulivan 11-14-1868 (11-24-1868)
Lankford, D. H. to Keziah Hay 6-14-1865 (6-15-1865)
Lankford, John N. H. to Margaret E. Marsh 5-10-1861
Lankford, L. D. J. to Harriet M. Parker 7-16-1860 (7-19-1860)
Lankford, Wm. to L. Hutchison 8-13-1859 (8-22-1859)
Lappay?, James to Mary Gilland 1-6-1866 (1-7-1866)
Larkins, B. F. to Mary D. Thompson 11-10-1869
Larkins, J. H. to E. F. Corliew 9-4-1866 (9-5-1866)
Larkins, Jno. J. to Franky H. Hooper 8-14-1858 (8-15-1858)
Larkins, Lewis to Docia Thompson 12-7-1867
Larkins, S. P. to Louisa P. Dunnagan 7-18-1866 (7-19-1866)
Larkins, Thos. B. to Elizabeth Hooper 11-25-1861 (11-26-1861)
Latour, Geo. to Mary Story 8-7-1864 (8-8-1864)
Laurence, W. H. H. to M. C. Russell 7-1-1865 (7-2-1865)
Lawrence, Joseph to Sarah Dowden 3-2-1870
Ledford, J. A. to Huldah McCrary 8-29-1864 (8-31-1864)
Lee, Wm. to Berdilla M. Mayfield 6-18-1859 (6-19-1859)
Leech, P. F. to J. W. Larkins 3-26-1861
Lewis, F. W. R. to Mary Ann Baldwin 8-10-1860 (8-12-1860)
Lewis, G. W. L. to S. J. Hays 3-28-1859 (3-31-1859)
Lewis, J. N. to M. F. Givens 1-24-1863 (1-28-1863)
Lewis, James to Mary Ann Whitfield 1-19-1867
Lewis, W. L. to F. E. Singleton 9-16-1870 (9-8?-1870)
Lewis, William to Jenny Thompson 9-24-1869 (9-26-1869)
Lile, Thos. to Sarah C. Jarman 7-2-1864
Lindsey, John to Minerva Hunter 5-13-1868
Lindsey, Leroy R. to Penina Kephart 12-28-1859 (1-8-1860)
Linsey, Wm. H. to Martha Ann Hegwood 3-5-1866 (3-6-1866)
Linzy, James M. to Elizabeth Woodward 2-2-1867 (2-3-1867)
Loftis, Geo. to Eddy King 2-21-1862 (2-23-1862)
Loftis, M. V. to S. E. Dunnagan 7-26-1859 (7-28-1859)
Loftis, V. S. to Sarah M. Graham 12-11-1865
Loggins, William J. to Sarah J. Dodson 1-20-1869 (1-21-1869)
Lomax, William to Clementine Dotson 7-27-1860 (8-2-1860)
Lona, John to Nacy R. Lawrence 3-31-1863 (4-2-1863)
Long, Alfred to M. A. Binkley 8-27-1870 (8-28-1870)
Long, George to Sarah Corlew 12-15-1866 (12-16-1866)
Long, George to Sarah Corlew no date (with Dec 1866)
Long, James H. to Sarah E. Dodson 4-23-1868
Long, Wm. James to Mary J. Grymes 6-12-1860
Lovell, James P. to Nancy C. Hale 1-24-1867
Lufman, John T. to Eliza Dugger 9-17-1870
Luther, George W. to Anna Spears 8-10-1867 (8-11-1867)
Luther, J. M. to Virginia H. Porter 6-5-1865 (6-8-1865)
Luther, Jno. M. to Nancy Davidson 9-24-1862 (10-1-1862)
Luther, N. J. to M. A. Anglin 3-3-1866 (3-4-1866)
Luther, Wm. to Martha Ladd 12-15-1864
Luther, Wm. T. to C. T. Clardy 8-10-1864
Lyle, Simeon to Elizabeth Boyed 1-10-1868
Lyles, John to Nancy L. McGaw 7-10-1860 (7-11-1860)
Lyles, Thomas to Jane Henley 9-23-1862
Majors, D. S. to S. C. Grigsby 5-29-1867

Manley, D. to S. J. Nash 6-3-1864
Manley, Reuben to Susan Tatom 4-19-1858
Marlow, Geo. to C. Green 10-13-1860 (10-14-1860)
Marsh, A. to Ann Yates 11-12-1860 (11-29-1860)
Marsh, Cane J. to _____ _____ 4-7-1869 (4-8-1869)
Marsh, W. C. to Indiana Spencer 2-26-1861 (2-28-1861)
Martin, C. J. to Tennessee A. Dickson 1-1-1867 (12?-1-1866)
Martin, J. D. to Mattilda M England 12-17-1868 (12-20-1868)
Martin, J. F. to Eleanora Murrell 9-5-1867 (9-6-1867)
Martin, Jones D. to Gemima A. England 3-29-1858 (3-30-1858)
Martin, S. B. to Amanda Potts 9-10-1869 (9-15-1869)
Mathews, James to Sarah C. Mills 1-2-1858 (1-4-1858)
Mathis, J. M. to A. M. Mathis 10-17-1860 (10-21-1860)
Mathis, James to Nancy Stewart 8-28-1857 (8-29-1857)
Mathis, John to Rhoda Broils 11-11-1864
Mathis, W. R. to E. E. Adcock 4-14-1858 (4-15-1858)
Mathis, William J. to Sarah E. Larkins 9-10-1868
Matlock, Edward to Lucretia Choate 8-16-1861
Matlock, Robert to Mary Quarles 9-15-1869
May, John T. to Sarah E. England 12-3-1868
Mayberry, Wm. to Sarah McClelland 2-20-1858 (2-21-1858)
McBride, William C. to Martha E. Ragan 6-5-1866 (6-9-1866)
McCarty, Dennis to Jerusha Adcock 7-18-1863
McCaslin, Benjamin T. to Martha E. Nicks 12-20-1866
McCaslin, F. to Julia P. Kye 6-1-1863 (6-18-1863)
McClelland, J. M. to Ann J. Smith 12-22-1858 (12-23-1858)
McClelland, Robert H. to Martha S. Dodson 5-26-1868 (5-27-1868)
McClelland, W. J. to Ann Williams 3-27-1860
McClerkin, A. B. to M. J. Adams 12-15-1870
McCloud, G. W. to Sarah Chester 10-3-1868 (10-4-1868)
McClure, A. J. to Martha L. Walch 2-28-1861
McClurkan, John to Cora L. Patey 7-31-1857 (8-2-1857)
McClurken, Samuel B. to Nancy F. Adams 11-14-1867
McCoy, John to Margaret Murrell? 3-14-1857 (3-15-1857)
McGeehee, Richard M. to Margarett Sellars 12-16-1868 (12-20-1868)
McKinstrey, Alexr. to Bridget McTagill 4-11-1861
McLaughlin, Galvin to Mary T. Harris 9-24-1859 (9-28-1859)
McLaughlin, Isaac? to Jeniatta J. Goodrich 9-10-1859 (9-13-1859)
McLyea, T. B. to Brunette Choate 3-13-1865 (3-15-1865)
McMurrey, Thos. W. to Sophrona V. Schmittou 5-3-1860
McWilliams, John F. to Charlott B. Kinzer 3-11-1870
Means, Joseph to Mary E. Campbell 12-6-1869 (12-7-1869)
Meek, James to Nancy Sewell 7-5-1858
Meek, M. H. to Martha J. Gentry 2-25-1862
Michel, J. W. to M. M. V. Schmittou 10-17-1866
Miller, Charles to Martha V. Gray 7-25-1865 (7-26-1865)
Miller, P. A. to Sarah J. Dailey 11-24-1859 (11-27-1859)
Mills, Jos. L. to Mary J. Marsh 11-29-1862
Mirwell?, Burkett to Kizziah Adcock 1-6-1862 (1-9-1862)
Mitchel, J. R. to Marthy N. V. Schmittou 2-5-1867 (2-6-1867)
Mitchel, John W. to Victoria Lee 9-25-1867 (9-26-1867)
Mitchell, Albert S. to Sarah Mayberry 12-25-1867

Mitchell, David A. to S. W. Dickson 1-18-1869 (1-20-1869)
Mitchell, Geo. O. B. to Sarah Edwards 3-24-1860 (3-25-1860)
Mitchell, J. T. to Henrietta Taylor 7-3-1870
Mitchell, M. B. to Christiana Rains 8-20-1864 (8-21-1864)
Mitchell, Wash to Rebecca Hunter 12-18-1860 (12-23-1860)
Mitchell, William M. to Louisa Hunter 10-14-1867 (10-16-1867)
Mixon, C. T. to Matilda Mathis 9-19-1864
Monroe, E. D. to Martha J. Jackson 8-14-1862 (8-16-1862)
Monroe, L. G. to Beady Selvestes Bull 11-1-1870 (11-3-1870)
Moody, James M. to Margaret A. Blanks 12-22-1870
Moore, Bartley to Nellie Choate 10-8-1857 (10-10-1857)
Moore, Daniel to Martha Shelton 12-29-1857 (12-30-1857)
Moore, George R. to Mary M. Dilleha 4-17-1869 (4-18-1869)
Morgan, James A. to Elizabeth Wood 8-10-1865
Morris, James H. to Elizabeth Wilkes 3-14-1870 (3-17-1870)
Morris, Thos. C. to Martha E. Rye 11-28-1858
Morris?, Thos. C. to Sarah L. Bowker 12-29-1859
Morrisett, W. D. to F. E. Norris 8-15-1857
Morrison, J. N. to Mary S. Self 2-16-1869 (2-17-1869)
Moss, Frank to Dicey M. Moore 8-27-1857 (8-28-1857)
Mulky, G. M. to Elizabeth Gillin 8-8-1864 (8-11-1864)
Murphey, R. B. to Saphrona Morris 10-3-1857 (10-4-1857)
Murphy, W. L. to Louisa Woods 9-7-1870
Murrell, B. to M. F. Adcock 10-8-1864 (10-9-1864)
Murrell, Makins? to Calley Crawford 12-21-1867 (12-24-1867)
Murrell, Richard C. to Mary Ann Adcock 10-13-1857 (10-15-1857)
Murrell, Thomas E. to Mary An Adams 12-28-1867 (1-2-1868)
Myatt, James F. to Margaret Errington 11-3-1866 (11-8-1866)
Myatt, Kendrick to Cyntha J. Ross 6-8-1866 (6-10-1866)
Myatt, Spencer A. to Mary O. Horner 12-19-1866 (12-20-1866)
Myatt, W. J. to E. C. Clifton 11-21-1864 (11-27-1864)
Nall, James W. to Rebecca P. Yates 11-6-1865
Nalls, Lindon A. to Martha Sellars 1-3-1859
Napier, W. H. to Elizabeth Coleman 11-21-1857 (11-22-1857)
Naramore, E. H. to Sarah Mathis 12-10-1859 (12-23-1859)
Neblett, P. P. to Laura A. Lowe 6-29-1857 (6-30-1857)
Nesbett, A. J. to Lee A. Harbison 12-26-1857 (12-27-1857)
Nesbitt, Jos. to M. L. Parker 9-28-1863 (10-1-1863)
Nichol, L. S. to Eliza A. Fowler 11-20-1869 (11-21-1869)
Nicholas, Thomas to Ann Winfrey 3-2-1866 (3-5-1866)
Nichols, Geo. W. to A. J. Adkins 11-12-1862 (11-15-1862)
Nichols, J. K. to Angeline McClelland 1-29-1870 (1-30-1870)
Nicks, Augustin to Henrietta A. Harper 10-18-1870
Nicks, John to Sarah E. Vales 4-4-1859 (4-22-1859)
Nicks, N. P.? to E. A. Hudgins 3-22-1863
Nicks, T. L. to Malviny Corlew 2-13-1867
Nicks, Webb? to Harriet Joslin 12-24-1859 (12-29-1859)
Nisson, Wm. T. to Tennessee Jones 6-24-1870 (6-26-1870)
Norris, W. J. to Dolly J. Thompson 10-14-1865
O'Connell, John to Rachael E. Ashworth 12-14-1867
Oconell, John to M. M. Hall 2-25-1860 (2-26-1860)
Odell, David to Media Binkley 6-23-1864

Organ, W. M. to Angie Dickson 11-29-1859
Orgorman, F. B. to Lucy McKelvy 4-4-1865
Osbourn, E. D. to Sarah Luttrell 1-15?-1868
Overton, William T. to Amanda E. Larkins 1-26-1867 (1-27-1867)
Owen, Jos. to Paschall Roena 7-30-1862
Owens, James to Susan R. Murrell 5-28-1867 (5-29-1867)
Owens, James M. to Mary E. Porter 12-13-1860
Owens, John H. to Malvina Alsbrook 11-7-1866 (11-8-1866)
Pack, L. J. to Elizabeth Smith 2-11-1860 (2-2?-1860)
Pack, Lenno to Martha Whitfield 11-9-1869 (11-14-1869)
Pack, Leroy D. to Martha L. Sims 10-3-1859 (10-5-1859)
Page, Harvey to Rebecca P. Rooker 10-22-1860 (10-28-1860)
Parker, Daniel to Elizabeth Garton 10-25-1864 (10-18?-1864)
Parker, H. A. to Martha J. Spencer 12-29-1869 (12-30-1869)
Parker, James L. to Susanah C. Johnston 7-18-1867 (7-7?-1867)
Parker, Jos.? to Mary Lankford 1-2-1860 (1-5-1860)
Parker, Sylvester to Elizabeth A. Sinks? 9-29-1859
Parks, Hamilton to F. B. Hardin 11-13-1869 (11-14-1869)
Parrish, A. C. to E. C. James 1-16-1865 (1-17-1865)
Parrish, A. J. to Sallie Bell 1-31-1865 (2-2-1865)
Parrish, James H. to Martha J. Morrison 5-12-1869 (5-13-1869)
Parrotte, Thomas H. to Susan F. Albright 2-1-1869 (2-4-1869)
Patey, J. O. to Jane Godfrey 9-1-1870
Patten, Milton B. to Martha W. Jones 10-12-1859 (10-13-1859)
Patterson, David to Mary A. Robertson 6-4-1870
Patterson, James to Sarah Warden 12-3-1866 (12-4-1866)
Patterson, M. V. to Eliza J. Waynick 6-8-1861 (6-9-1861)
Patterson, Robert to S. C. Hampton 5-28-1870 (5-29-1870)
Patterson, S. to S. A. Proctor 12-23-1858
Patterson, Samuel to Hannah M. Harper 11-11-1870
Patton, J. to L. Perkins 6-3-1864 (10-27-1864)
Paty, Louis to Adeline Bruce 11-29-1858 (11-30-1858)
Payne, Zachree to Catharine E. A. Shelton 9-3-1867 (9-5-1867)
Pendergrass, W. A. to H. O. _____ 3-14-1863
Pendergrass, William E. to Hulda C. Sears 5-4-1867
Pendergrass, Wm. to Artamissa Anglin 11-18-1862
Perry, Eli to Mary C. Martin 7-16-1870 (7-17-1870)
Petty, A. J. to Charity Russell 8-13-1859
Petty, G. H. to M. A. Dunnagan 11-28-1866
Petty, Jackson to Perlina Petty 12-21-1868
Petty, John A. to C. T. Stinnett 7-31-1863
Petty, John S. to Charity J. Myatt 10-11-1870 (10-13-1870)
Petty, Levi S. to Susan A. Murrell 10-21-1861 (10-20?-1861)
Petty, S. H. to M. E. Marsh 1-27-1864 (1-28-1864)
Petty, Tho. D. to Adeline Vineyard 10-27-1858 (10-31-1858)
Petty, William M. to Mary C. Sugg 9-23-1868 (9-25-1868)
Picket, Henry to Elizabeth R. Harrell 4-13-1869 (4-14-1869)
Pickett, Henry E. to Susan A. E. Street 6-1-1859 (6-2-1859)
Pickett, J. J. to Jane Slayden 1-12-1861 (1-13-1861)
Pool, A. T. P. to Julia A. Rains 1-4-1863 (1-7-1863)
Porch, W. S. to Alice J. Street 8-21-1861 (9-4-1861)
Porter, J. K. to Susan M. Ross 11-9-1865

Potter, Shelby to sMary Ferrell 5-26-1870 (5-31-1870)
Potter, Solomon to Susan Carroll 9-1-1862
Potts, B. C. to Louisa Crow 5-5-1864
Potts, James F. to Mary E. O. (V.?) Schmittou 1-7-1857 (1-8-1857)
Potts, John M. to Alsey Ann V. Schmittou 5-7-1870 (5-17-1870)
Potts, W. R. to F. S. Blount 11-14-1861
Price, J. A. to Fanney Pernell 4-25-1857
Price, J. J. to Jane Hooper 11-16-1867 (11-20-1868?)
Price, Reuben to Ruth Howel 1-10-1865 (1-11-1865)
Price, T. J. to Amanda C. Adams 1-27-1870
Prichard, Benjamin to Sarah Sellars 3-23-1870 (3-24-1870)
Priest, J. J. to Delia Philips 2-9-1867 (2-10-1867)
Prockter, Thomas O. to Mary E. Wall 8-2-1869 (8-6-1869)
Proctor, Henderson to Darcus Musgroves 4-10-1858 (4-11-1858)
Puett, George M. to Julia F. Herbison 10-24-1867 (10-27-1867)
Ragain, Geo. to Sarah J. Gilmore 10-20-1863 (10-22-1863)
Rawls, Jackson to Harriet M. Garton 8-8-1862
Ray, A. W. to H. B. Payne 9-26-1863 (9-27-1863)
Ray, Isaac to Holly B. Bramlet 5-30-1868 (6-7-1868)
Raymond, William N. to Thankful J. Milam 11-2-1867 (11-3-1867)
Reaves, John A. J. to Bettie A. Proctor 11-8-1860
Reed, Isaac to Arminta E. Dugger 5-24-1870
Reed, W. C. to Lorena White 12-26-1866 (12-28-1866)
Reep, Soloman to Jane McCreary 4-12-1870 (4-19-1870)
Register, Thomas S. to Mary A. Luther 10-31-1868
Reynolds, John L. to M. E. Singleton 12-29-1870
Reynolds, M. V. to Mary C. Crockett 2-27-1858
Reynolds, W. A. to M. A. Albright 6-16-1865 (6-18-1865)
Reynolds, W. R. to Mary Welker 6-4-1866 (6-7-1866)
Rice, David H. to Eliza J. Tidwell 5-21-1861
Rice, William H. to Anna T. Parrish 12-11-1867 (12-17-1867)
Richardson, Batty to Tennessee A. Thompson 10-8-1870 (10-9-1870)
Richardson, John W. to Mary T. Oakley 2-10-1858 (2-13-1858)
Richardson, W. T. to Catharine Alspaugh 1-16-1866 (1-17-1866)
Robbins, W. P. to C. E. Gamble 8-17-1861
Roberson, J. D. to Frances C. Newman 6-30-1866 (7-1?-1866)
Roberson, J. M. to Ellenory Paty 2-8-1866
Roberson, W. W. to Tennie Gilmore 9-16-1867 (9-17-1867)
Roberts, William R. to Mary Heard 7-20-1867 (7-31-1867)
Robertson, D. G. to M. J. Newmon 7-19-1864
Robertson, David to Mary M. Gilmore 7-30-1868
Robertson, J. K. to Bettie Adams 10-18-1866
Robinson, Abner to Alcey A. Street 1-3-1860 (1-11-1860)
Robinson, Charley to E. A. Davidson 3-29-1858 (3-30-1858)
Rogers, J. B. to Nancy J. Dunn 7-9-1863
Rogers, John to Amanda Tatom 12-28-1870 (12-29-1870)
Rose, C. G. H. to Mallinda Hatley 7-31-1869
Rose, R. H. to S. L. Nick 12-23-1863
Rose, Van T. to Adline Parmer 9-6-1865
Rosser, G. S. to Mary E. England 9-7-1867 (9-11-1867)
Rowland, J. S. to M. A. Adams 12-6-1863
Runnells, Geo. W. to Geo. A. D. Runnells 5-23-1862 (5-25-1862)

Runnols, Samuel to Emily Crockett 11-13-1866 (11-14-1866)
Runyan, S. C. to Elizer Mathis 1-11-1866 (1-21-1866)
Russell, J. H. to Rebecca Patterson 1-27-1862 (1-29-1862)
Russell, J. M. to Tennessee J. Dillaha 11-25-1868 (11-26-1868)
Russell, John A. J. to Jemima Owens 7-4-1860
Russell, L. S. to P. L. Richardson 11-22-1858 (11-23-1858)
Russell, Wiley M. to Sarah M. Sugg 12-9-1867
Russell, William to Frances Pack 5-18-1860
Rutledge, Sterling to Louisa J. Brazzell 8-27-1857 (8-28-1857)
Rutlege, Marion to Mary Martha Porter 1-11-1866 (1-12-1866)
Rye, A. B. to Nancy A. Biter (Seals) 3-20-1861
Rye, John to Gemima Humphreys 6-12-1858 (6-13-1858)
Sampson, F. M. to Amanda Jones 10-5-1869 (10-6-1869)
Sanders, John J. to M. J. Fussell 12-30-1869
Sanders, John S. to Mary Turnidge 1-22-1864 (1-24-1864)
Sanders, Thomas B. to Margarett Walker 12-31-1868
Schmittou, G. D. V. to Nancy C. Martin 1-31-1857 (2-3-1857)
Schmittou, J. C. to Mary M. Stark 9-17-1868 (9-20-1868)
Scott, St Clair to Dilly Speight 10-28-1859 (2-18-1861)
Scott, William C. to Parlee J. Hunter 9-4-1869 (9-2?-1869)
Seals, Jacob to Rutha A. C. Hays 8-30-1857
Seals, P T. to Nancy Ann Jones 5-26-1870
Searcy, R. to Nannie M. Heggie 2-20-1862 (4-2-1862)
Sears, Jas. to Susan Spencer 7-6-1864 (7-7-1864)
Sears, John to Jane Glass 8-8-1868 (8-9-1868)
Sears, John to Rebecca Sears 1-21-1865 (1-22-1865)
Sears, R. F. to Nancy A. Adcock 4-5-1864 (4-7-1864)
Seels, Geo. W. to Elizabeth Seals 2-1-1862
Self, A. to O. T. Adams 12-20-1858 (12-21-1858)
Sellars, John J. to Clara Garton 10-13-1859 (10-2?-1859)
Sellars, John J. to Harriett P. Carr 11-20-1865 (11-23-1865)
Sensing, A. B. to G. A. Harris 3-6-1867
Sensing, John E. to Elizabeth E. Hays 6-20-1859
Sensing, John H. to H. B. Payne 12-27-1860
Sensing, W. P. to Lucy B. Gilmore 11-28-1861
Sesler, Thomas to Tennessee Jackson 7-7-1862 (7-15-1862)
Sestler, Wm. H. to Susan E. Heath 9-15-1865 (11-14-1865)
Shaw, W. A. to E. A. Dunnaway 1-26-1858
Shelton, J. W. J. to Sarah Ann Work 12-6-1869 (12-9?-1869)
Shelton, Joab L. to Missouri E. Thompson 2-11-1867
Shelton, W. J. to E.J. Sweaney 8-12-1870 (8-14-1870)
Shmittou, J. B. V. to Mary E. Reynolds 11-7-1866
Shufield?, Nicholas to Elizabeth Hunter 1-16-1861 (1-20-1861)
Sills, Saml? to Jane Gregory 2-14-1861
Simpson, William J. to Rebecca P. Myatt 11-?-1867
Sinks, William A. to Mary Ann Crane 5-10-1867 (5-12-1867)
Sisler, Henry to Nancy? C. Adcock 8-3-1869 (8-6-1869)
Skelton, Jas. M. to Lenora Shelton 2-14-1865 (2-15-1865)
Slayden, J. R. to S. A. Green 1-18-1863 (1-19-1863)
Smith, A. J. to Bettie G. Daniel 2-3-1869
Smith, D. G. to India A. Vanhook 4-5-1869 (4-11-1869)
Smith, G. W. to Louisa Taylor 11-7-1857 (11-8-1857)

Smith, Henry C. to Fredonia C. Norris 11-2-1869 (11-7-1869)
Smith, J. D. to C. C. Adcock 11-11-1863 (11-22-1863)
Smith, J. N. to E. A. Scott 10-3-1864 (10-6-1864)
Smith, James to Emily Pendergrass 11-18-1870 (11-20-1870)
Smith, Jas. M. to Mary A. Hunter 3-16-1864 (3-17-1864)
Smith, John A. to Martha C. Spradling 9-3-1868
Smith, R. P. to K. P. Shelton 2-20-1866
Smith, Uriah to Ann Qualls 7-5-1864
Smith, W. H. to Josephine Dunnagan 8-6-1870 (8-7-1870)
Smith, William H. to Elizabeth Mathis 6-29-1868 (7-1-1868)
Smothers, Wiley to Rebecca Chaudoin 1-13-1864 (1-14-1864)
Southerland, Geo. W. to Amanda Rooker 12-4-1860
Spann, S. H. to Lucy J. Averitt 5-12-1866 (5-13-1866)
Spears, T. C. to S. E. Clardy 10-13-1860 (10-14-1860)
Speight, Jesse B. to Ellen M. Williams 9-28-1868 (9-29-1868)
Speight, Westley to Martha Elizabeth Andrews 8-7-1865 (8-13-1865)
Spencer, Hyram to Celia Sowells 2-5-1857
Spicer, O. C. to Tennessee Garton 11-16-1861 (11-17-1861)
Spicer, Tho. to Susan F. Daniel 10-8-1862 (10-9-1862)
Spradlin, O. M. to Mahala J. Booker 5-28-1865
Springer, John A. to Sarah E. Woody 9-1-1868
Springer, Jos. T. to Sarah O. Evans 1-19-1857 (1-20-1857)
Spurlock, John to Amanda E. Balthrop 4-23-1859 (4-24-1859)
Stanfill, J. F. to Susan P. Adkins 5-5-1868 (5-7-1868)
Stanton, P. F. to Elizabeth Black 1-7-1863
Stark, Thos. to E. H. Weakley 5-6-1864
Steel, James to Parmelia Sanders 2-14-1867
Steel, R. D. to S. E. Redden 12-1-1866 (12-6-1866)
Steele, Robt. to Sarah McCollum 5-2-1861
Stewart, J. R. to Sallie M. Hall 11-12-1868
Stewart, Jno. C. to Martha Mathis 8-25-1858 (8-28-1858)
Stewart, Noah to Martha Mathews 6-9-1857 (6-11-1857)
Stockard, A. C. to Mary Jane Larkins 11-2-1865
Stokes, J. M. to Olive J. Kellum 1-20-1868 (1-21-1868)
Stokes, Wiley M. to Victoria E. Pentecost 2-11-1868 (2-13-1868)
Stokey, William W. to Malissa Redings 4-27-1867 (4-28-1867)
Stone, Robert B. to Sarah M. Jackson 1-21-1868 (1-22-1868)
Story, Melvin W. to Margaret Edwards 11-11-1867
Story, Oatis to Mary Cooley 3-12-1859 (3-13-1859)
Story, Samuel H. to Rebecca Waller 7-22-1869
Street, D. W. to Pauline Anglin 9-11-1866
Street, H. W. to Elizer F. Street 8-26-1867 (12-27-1867)
Street, R. F. to Virginia Parmenter 5-4-1868 (5-7-1868)
Stroud, A. N. to E. V. O. Matlock 11-19-1870
Stuart, J. M. to Clarisa Spicer 12-27-1865
Sugg, John D. to Cary Jane Springer 4-3-1857 (4-7-1857)
Sullivan, Andrew J. to Sarah J. Tidwell 7-14-1870 (7-17-1870)
Sullivan, Jas. H. to G. A. P. Latham 1-16-1865 (1-18-1865)
Sullivan, Jos. to Penny? Tidwell 1-19-1860 (1-22-1860)
Summer, Dempsey to Anelizer Hall 12-1-1866 (12-2-1866)
Sweeny, J. G. to Martha S. Hale 12-14-1858 (12-15-1858)
Swift, A. to M. A. Mixon 8-19-1864 (8-20-1864)

Swift, G. W. to M. C. Kenedy 12-23-1867 (12-24-1867)
Swift, James T. to M. E. Dickson 4-11-1859
Talley, J. L. to Martha W. Walker 9-27-1865
Talley, J. M. to Catharine McCauley 1-1-1868
Tate?, Tho. N. to Mary F. Adcock 12-28-1858 (12-29-1858)
Tatom, E. J. to Susan Carrington 9-8-1858 (9-9-1858)
Tatom, Geo. to Martha Bowen 1-15-1862 (1-26-1862)
Tatom, M. B. to Frances Allspaugh 12-12-1862 (12-16-1862)
Tatom, W. B. to A. M. F. Nicholl 4-7-1858 (4-8-1858)
Tatom, W. B. to E. J. Miller 10-30-1858
Tatom, W. B. to Frances Hibbs 9-10-1866 (9-11-1866)
Taylor, Benj. (Berry?) to Eliza H. Ball 1-28-1861 (1-29-1861)
Taylor, Henry to Malinda Edwards 8-8-1866 (8-12-1866)
Taylor, J.? R.? to Elizabeth Naibers? 3-12-1863
Taylor, John to Matilda Glassgo 1-17-1857
Taylor, John Q. to Mary S. Hall 1-26-1867 (1-27-1867)
Taylor, Jos. to P. A. Ford 3-19-1861 (3-20-1861)
Taylor, M. to N.? C. Gilmore 1-30-1864
Taylor, Tho. to Rebecca Biter 12-26-1857
Taylor, Thomas to Susan A. Thompson 11-10-1869
Taylor, W. H. to Mary Richardson 1-16-1868
Taylor, Webb S. to Elizabeth Creech 11-30-1869 (12-5-1869)
Taylor, Wm. to Mary A. Nalls 6-29-1865
Thomas, H. C. to Tessa Garton 2-17-1858
Thomas, John H. to Mary L. Haney 5-4-1866
Thomason, James to M. J. Lloyd 5-4-1857 (5-10-1857)
Thompson, Epps J. to Mary Ann Karns 9-21-1859 (9-22-1859)
Thompson, Henry W. to Mary J. McMahan 8-25-1869
Thompson, Jeremiah to Emily J. Thompson 4-5-1859
Thompson, William A. to C. E. Craft 5-11-1867
Thompson, William T. to Martha E. Yates 9-2-1868
Tibbs, J. M. to Maliss Jane Ragan 10-16-1869 (10-17-1869)
Tidwell, Aquilla to Rebecca Russell 12-14-1859 (12-15-1859)
Tidwell, E. J. to E. A. Nash 1-17-1865
Tidwell, Edmond M. to Amanda Tate 2-24-1859
Tidwell, Edward to Ann Rainey 6-23-1858
Tidwell, F. M. to Martha Sullivan 11-3-1857
Tidwell, John H. to Elizabeth Underhill 10-17-1859
Tidwell, Jonah (Josiah?) to Elizabeth Sellars 2-11-1862 (2-12-1862)
Tidwell, S. A. to Sarah J. Johnston 7-20-1870
Tidwell, S. M. to Lucinda Garton 2-5-1867 (2-7-1867)
Tidwell, Wilson to Martha Lampley 2-4-1860 (2-12-1860)
Tilly, Henderson to Ellen C. Choate 7-28-1858
Tinley, Thos. to Ann Ethilliams 12-28-1860 (1-1-1861)
Tipton, Robt. M. to Sarah J. Naramore 5-7-1864 (5-11-1864)
Toler, G. W. to Nancy Ann Mathews 7-6-1867
Trammel, James to Sarah Loftis 1-5-1857 (1-19-1857)
True, Richard C. to Susan C. Gust? 12-7-1860
Tubb, W. C. to M. M. Walker 1-21-1863
Tucker, John W. to Sarah J. Dunnagan 7-18-1860 (7-22-1860)
Tucker, W. T. to M.J. Kirk 6-1-1857 (6-2-1857)
Tummons, James to Elizabeth J. Adams 3-21-1866 (3-22-1866)

Tummons, Joseph to Margaret Dotson 3-29-1866
Tummons?, William R. to Martha Bagwell 10-3-1867
Turner, A. G. to M. E. Bledsoe 7-7-1863 (7-18-1863)
Turner, D. D. to Lydia Simmons? 7-20-1863 (7-24-1863)
Turner, John J. to M. E. Ragan 9-7-1864 (9-8-1864)
Turner, John J. to Mary A. Arnold 8-27-1859 (8-28-1859)
Turner, R. G. to M. J. Cocke 9-16-1863
Turner, W. to Mary Pickett 10-16-1865
Turner, W. V. to L. M. Skelton 8-4-1864
Underwood, Henry to Melvina E. Ferrel 3-8-1862 (3-6?-1862)
Underwood, Th. W. to A. O. Climer 6-13-1857 (6-14-1858?)
Vale, W. H. to Ann Taylor 2-2-1859
Vance, James F. to Martha J. Weems 12-26-1868 (12-27-1868)
Vanhook, Wm. to Mary Thompson 11-25-1861
Vanwanner, Oscar to Sarah J. Satterfield no date (with Mar 1866)
Vineyard, Corder to Nancy J. Baker 7-31-1861 (8-4-1861)
Vinyard, A. R. to M. E. Phillips 9-18-1860
Vinyard, M. H. to Rebeca J. England 8-21-1866 (8-30-1866)
Walker, B. F. to Harriet M. Shivers? 12-11-1858 (12-12-1858)
Walker, James M. to Nancy L. Willey 7-15-1869
Walker, Levi V. to Mary A. Cockmen 12-27-1857 (12-30-1857)
Walker, Robt. to Anna Tidwell 11-13-1860 (11-22-1860)
Walker, Samuel T. to Elinora? F. Paty 2-5-1867 (2-14-1867)
Walker, Thos. R. B. to V. C. E. Berry 5-21-1868
Wall, H. B. to Margaret E. Prockter 11-2-1867 (11-3-1867)
Wallace, A. J. to Mary L. Bone 11-30-1866 (12-2-1866)
Wallace, Andrew to Mary Mathis 7-28-1857
Wallace, David to Susan Patterson 3-2-1857 (3-3-1857)
Waller, W. T. to Arminday Jane Edwards 4-15-1870 (4-19-1870)
Waller, W. T. to Malissa Willey 10-4-1862 (10-5-1862)
Ward, John S. to Eunice A. Robertson 4-21-1859
Ward, M. to Sarah Noughton 11-18-1861 (11-20-1861)
Warwick, Charles W. to Lucy A. Estes 2-23?-1868
Waska, Jas. to Adaline Benife? 1-14-1865 (1-15-1865)
Watkin, W. E. to Lucy Gray 8-3-1863 (8-6-1863)
Weakley, John A. to Martha A. Mayberry 10-6-1868 (10-3?-1868)
Weakley, W. S. to Martha E. Hodges 3-3-1858
Weaver, John H. to Nancy A. J. Lea 9-7-1868 (9-10-1868)
Weemes, W. L. to Louisa M. Lankford 1-17-1867
Weems, Corder T. to Arminta Dunnagan 10-25-1869
Weems, W. T. to Louisa P. Langford 1-31-1866
Welch, John to Susan Garton 8-12-1867 (8-14-1867)
Wells, E. to M. Adcock 8-8-1859
Wells, Eli to F. C. Bowen 4-7-1857 (4-9-1857)
Wells, John H. to M. M. Bell 10-9-1860
Wells, S. J. A. to Ellen D. Holt 4-26-1858
White, C. D. to Mary Jane Pickett 1-26-1870 (1-27-1870)
White, Daniel to Caroline Parker 11-4-1862
White, Henry to Mary Alsbrooks 11-5-1870 (11-10-1870)
White, James to Sarah Elizabeth Ford 4-17-1867
White, M. W. to Sarah C. Adcock 12-22-1870
White, W. M. to M. A. Prichett 11-16-1866 (11-26-1866)

White?, B. C. to C. O. Lavis? 3-14-1863
Whitfield, Thomas to Mary Jones 3-7-1867 (3-10-1867)
Whitlock, Thomas to Sarah Tatom 11-5-1866 (11-7-1866)
Wilber, A. W. to Pauline L. Hopely 12-23-1865 (12-24-1865)
Williams, A. J. to Fredonia Hagwood 5-12-1868
Williams, B. R. to Pheba A. Corlew 9-23-1857
Williams, David R. to Indiana Gilbert 2-14-1860
Williams, Denny R. to Harriet Perry 4-9-1866
Williams, Ed to Mary Gillan 4-29-1865 (4-30-1865)
Williams, G. A. to M. F. Street 9-28-1863 (9-29-1863)
Williams, G. C. to A. A. Jones 8-31-1870 (9-1-1870)
Williams, H. W. to Sarah J. Carrell 11-10-1866 (11-12-1866)
Williams, J. B. to Sarah ann Harris 8-24-1865
Williams, J. G. to Lucretia C. Choate 12-16-1865
Williams, J. N. to Jennie Mathews 2-4-1864
Williams, J. W. to Harriet Prockter 9-8-1869 (9-10-1869)
Williams, James to E. Rogers 10-27-1863
Williams, James F. to Mary Jane McCormack 10-8-1870 (10-9-1870)
Williams, James R. to Mary M. Street 9-8-1858 (no return)
Williams, Joel to Eliza J. Rutlage 11-25-1869
Williams, John W. to Sarah Ann Matlock 8-20-1870 (8-21-1870)
Williams, Joseph to Retly? England 9-17-1866
Williams, Robert P. to Lucy R. Woodward 2-12-1870 (2-13-1870)
Williams, William E. to Atalanta V. Stroud 3-17-1869 (3-18-1869)
Wills, S. J. A. to Lotty Tatom 1-31-1865 (2-5-1865)
Wilson, J. P. to E. A. Adams 11-18-1861 (11-21-1861)
Winfrey, Walter S. to Manervy E. Deasant 2-16-1866 (3-4-1866)
Winick, G. J. to Jemimah Paterson 8-5-1865 (8-7-1865)
Winstead, Saml. A. to Sarah M. Adams 1-25-1857
Woodward, Theophilus to Emeline Chadwick 9-3-1868
Woody, William S. to Mary E. Baker 9-21-1868
Woollund, Alexander to Ritha S. Walker 12-27-1862 (12-28-1862)
Wooten, A. W. to Elizabeth D. Nesbitt 8-28-1869 (10-5-1869)
Work, Egbert to Mary Whitlock 6-30-1868 (7-?-1868)
Work, Jno. H. to E. J. Redden 11-21-1861 (11-24-1861)
Work, Joseph A. to Sophia Shelton 5-26-1868
Work, T. J. to Palistrue Redden 2-1-1870 (2-3-1870)
Yates, A. J. to Sarah E. Johnson 6-30-1866 (7-5-1866)
Yates, Brittain to Laminty Pistol 10-29-1860 (10-30-1860)
Yates, C. R. to F. H. Myatt 1-13-1865
Yates, Isaac O. to Mary J. Myatt 8-15-1868 (8-16-1868)
Yates, James to E. T. (Mrs.) Greer 3-28-1862 (3-30-1862)
Yates, James H. to Artela Tate 1-8-1870
Yates, John to Mary Bowen 1-1-1857 (1-4-1857)
Yates, Jos. to Sarah Brown 11-30-1861 (12-1-1861)
Yates, Thos. B. to Mary K. Haley 2-24-1865 (2-26-1865)
Yates, William to Elizabeth Cathey 8-10-1867 (8-11-1867)
Yeates, W. M. to Sophia Goodrich 11-25-1857 (12-8-1857)
Young, James to Susan Albert 8-21-1869 (8-22-1869)
Young, John to Elizabeth Joslin 11-18-1869
Young, Thos. S. to Louisa J. Hunter 12-25-1858 (12-26-1858)

Adams, Amanda C. to T. J. Price 1-27-1870
Adams, Bettie to J. K. Robertson 10-18-1866
Adams, E. A. to J. P. Wilson 11-18-1861 (11-21-1861)
Adams, Elizabeth J. to James Tummons 3-21-1866 (3-22-1866)
Adams, M. A. to J. S. Rowland 12-6-1863
Adams, M. J. to A. B. McClerkin 12-15-1870
Adams, Martha Ann to James H. Brown 8-16-1867 (8-17-1867)
Adams, Mary A. to John Adams 9-13-1858 (9-14-1858)
Adams, Mary An to Thomas E. Murrell 12-28-1867 (1-2-1868)
Adams, Nancy F. to Samuel B. McClurken 11-14-1867
Adams, O. T. to A. Self 12-20-1858 (12-21-1858)
Adams, Rebecca J. to A. Abercrombie 1-11-1866
Adams, Sarah M. to Saml. A. Winstead 1-25-1857
Adcock, C. C. to J. D. Smith 11-11-1863 (11-22-1863)
Adcock, E. E. to W. R. Mathis 4-14-1858 (4-15-1858)
Adcock, Jerusha to Dennis McCarty 7-18-1863
Adcock, Kizziah to Burkett Mirwell? 1-6-1862 (1-9-1862)
Adcock, Lucindy A. to Jesse H. Adcock 1-?-1868
Adcock, M. to E. Wells 8-8-1859
Adcock, M. F. to B. Murrell 10-8-1864 (10-9-1864)
Adcock, Martha A. to R. Goodwin 2-24-1859
Adcock, Mary Ann to Richard C. Murrell 10-13-1857 (10-15-1857)
Adcock, Mary F. to Tho. N. Tate? 12-28-1858 (12-29-1858)
Adcock, Mary S. to J. C. Dunnagan 1-10-1869
Adcock, Nancy A. to R. F. Sears 4-5-1864 (4-7-1864)
Adcock, Nancy? C. to Henry Sisler 8-3-1869 (8-6-1869)
Adcock, Polly A. to M. R. Crow 12-6-1858 (12-7-1858)
Adcock, Sarah C. to M. W. White 12-22-1870
Adkins, A. J. to Geo. W. Nichols 11-12-1862 (11-15-1862)
Adkins, Martha A. to J. E. Craig 9-2-1868 (9-3-1868)
Adkins, Susan P. to J. F. Stanfill 5-5-1868 (5-7-1868)
Albert, Susan to James Young 8-21-1869 (8-22-1869)
Albright, M. A. to W. A. Reynolds 6-16-1865 (6-18-1865)
Albright, Susan F. to Thomas H. Parrotte 2-1-1869 (2-4-1869)
Allbright, Eliza J. to James H. Hassell 5-10-1870 (5-18-1870)
Allbright, Sallie M. to Wm. C. Baker 10-12-1866 (10-14-1866)
Allison, Nannie to Hugh Allison 2-13-1858 (2-16-1858)
Allspaugh, Frances to M. B. Tatom 12-12-1862 (12-16-1862)
Alsbrook, Malvina to John H. Owens 11-7-1866 (11-8-1866)
Alsbrooks, Mary to Henry White 11-5-1870 (11-10-1870)
Alspaugh, Catharine to W. T. Richardson 1-16-1866 (1-17-1866)
Anderson, Sarah to Jesse M. Ford 3-6-1866
Andrews, Martha Elizabeth to Westley Speight 8-7-1865 (8-13-1865)
Anglin, A. J. to J. H. Hudson 1-5-1866 (1-9-1866)
Anglin, Artamissa to Wm. Pendergrass 11-18-1862
Anglin, Louisa E. to W. G. L. Buttrey 7-27-1866 (7-31-1866)
Anglin, M. A. to N. J. Luther 3-3-1866 (3-4-1866)
Anglin, Pauline to D. W. Street 9-11-1866
Arnold, Mary A. to John J. Turner 8-27-1859 (8-28-1859)

Ashworth, Rachael E. to John O'Connell 12-14-1867
Austin, Elizabeth Catharine to A. N. Austin 12-4-1865 (12-5-1865)
Austin, Lucinda P. to James R. Frasher 2-11-1858
Austin, Martha Ann to Isaac Bateman 7-2-1870
Averitt, Lucy J. to S. H. Spann 5-12-1866 (5-13-1866)
Ayers, Elenory to Monroe Brown 5-28-1870
Ayers, Hetty E. to E. W. Giddings 5-11-1870 (5-19-1870)
Bagwell, Martha to William R. Tummons? 10-3-1867
Bailey, M. P. to A. B. Browning 12-29-1865 (12-30-1865)
Baker, Eliza Jane to Geo. Lamastus 8-12-1857 (8-13-1857)
Baker, Isabel to George W. Hassel 5-26-1869 (5-30-1869)
Baker, M. C. to R. G. England 12-20-1866
Baker, Margarett C. to J. F. Furgerson 12-29-1869
Baker, Mary E. to John A. Doty 12-20-1870 (12-21-1870)
Baker, Mary E. to H. W. Haley 10-28-1861 (11-7-1861)
Baker, Mary E. to William S. Woody 9-21-1868
Baker, Mary J. to F. M. Allbrooks 3-14-1861
Baker, Missouri to Thomas W. Burn 12-27-1868
Baker, Nancy J. to Corder Vineyard 7-31-1861 (8-4-1861)
Baker, S. E. to J. L. Chilton 1-19-1864
Baker, Sarah E. to J.? L. Chilton 8-19?-1865
Baldwin, Mary Ann to F. W. R. Lewis 8-10-1860 (8-12-1860)
Baldwin, Missouri J. to John J. Hughs 10-7-1857
Baldwin, Nancy J. to John H. Briant 12-27-1860
Baldwin, Tennessee to J. M. Briant 12-24-1869
Ball, Eliza H. to Benj. (Berry?) Taylor 1-28-1861 (1-29-1861)
Ballard, Jennetta G. to John Holley 1-2-1866 (1-7-1866)
Balthrop, Amanda E. to John Spurlock 4-23-1859 (4-24-1859)
Barns, Sarah R. P. to James W. Gray 7-25-1860 (7-26-1860)
Bell, M. M. to John H. Wells 10-9-1860
Bell, Sallie to A. J. Parrish 1-31-1865 (2-2-1865)
Benife?, Adaline to Jas. Waska 1-14-1865 (1-15-1865)
Berry, V. C. E. to Thos. R. B. Walker 5-21-1868
Binkley, M. A. to Alfred Long 8-27-1870 (8-28-1870)
Binkley, Media to David Odell 6-23-1864
Bishop, Mary to Wm. R. Kee 8-5-1864
Bishop, Mary E. to Andrew J. Lampley 7-4-1862 (7-13-1862)
Bishop, Nancy to John Black 7-8-1864
Bishop, Sarah E. to James M. Bowker (Booker?) 5-14-1870 (5-15-1870)
Biter, Rebecca to Tho. Taylor 12-26-1857
Biter (Seals), Nancy A. to A. B. Rye 3-20-1861
Black, Elizabeth to P. F. Stanton 1-7-1863
Blackwell, Sarah M. to McKenzy S. Hays 1-27-1870
Blanks, Margaret A. to James M. Moody 12-22-1870
Bledsoe, M. E. to A. G. Turner 7-7-1863 (7-18-1863)
Bledsow, H. F. to A. H. Bone 11-18-1864 (11-20-1864)
Blount, F. S. to W. R. Potts 11-14-1861
Bond, Catherine to Jiles Adams 4-2-1866
Bone, Mary L. to A. J. Wallace 11-30-1866 (12-2-1866)
Bone, Sarah Elizabeth to Robert A. Hudson 5-19-1866 (5-20-1866)

Booker, Mahala J. to O. M. Spradlin 5-28-1865
Booze, Virginia A. to Turner Halliburton 11-7-1866 (11-8-1866)
Bowen, Bettie to J. F. Conklin 4-29-1868
Bowen, F. C. to Eli Wells 4-7-1857 (4-9-1857)
Bowen, Fannie E. to J. G. Jones 12-28-1870
Bowen, Margaret R. to T. C. Jarnagan 6-28-1869 (7-8-1869)
Bowen, Martha to Geo. Tatom 1-15-1862 (1-26-1862)
Bowen, Mary to John Yates 1-1-1857 (1-4-1857)
Bowen, P. J. to W. J. Jones 8-16-1865 (8-17-1865)
Bowen, Susan A. to Robert Booker 11-20-1858 (11-21-1858)
Bower, R. J. to Tho. Halliburton 8-15-1857 (8-16-1857)
Bowker, Sarah L. to Thos. C. Morris? 12-29-1859
Boyed, Elizabeth to Simeon Lyle 1-10-1868
Bramlet, Holly B. to Isaac Ray 5-30-1868 (6-7-1868)
Bramlet, Laury to Will Hendrix 12-3-1869 (12-5-1869)
Brazzel, M. P. to J. L. Jackson 5-31-1865 (6-1-1865)
Brazzell, Louisa J. to Sterling Rutledge 8-27-1857 (8-28-1857)
Brazzell, Nancy E. to W. C. Hatcher 2-1-1870 (2-3-1870)
Briant, Martha A. to James A. Carrell 9-11-1869 (9-12-1869)
Broils, Rhoda to John Mathis 11-11-1864
Brown, Bettie to Griffith Garton 4-17-1869
Brown, F. C. to James R. Dunnagan 10-23-1858 (10-24-1858)
Brown, Louisa to Joseph Karns 12-17-1864 (12-18-1864)
Brown, Lucindy M. to E. N. Cathey 2-10-1866 (2-11-1866)
Brown, Marry A. to W. H. Lamastis 3-15-1866
Brown, Mary to Ben F. Hall 3-19-1862 (3-20-1862)
Brown, Mary to James Hayse 1-16-1869 (1-17-1869)
Brown, Mary E. to Jno. M. Hay 3-15-1861 (3-17-1861)
Brown, R. L. to J. B. Henry 5-3-1869 (5-6-1869)
Brown, Sarah to George W. Baker 7-18-1866 (7-21-1866)
Brown, Sarah to Jos. Yates 11-30-1861 (12-1-1861)
Brown, Susan to Ben Jordan 1-2-1860 (1-3-1860)
Brown, Susan E. to Archabald Cathey 2-1-1860
Browning, Mencacy? to Chas. Halliburton 12-25-1860 (1-13-1861)
Browning, Sarah to Thos. L. T. Dickson 7-22-1858 (7-25-1858)
Bruce, Adeline to Louis Paty 11-29-1858 (11-30-1858)
Bryant, N. E. to D. J. Bryant 1-22-1863
Bryant, Sarah to Joel Errington 10-28-1867 (11-29-1867)
Bull, Beady Selvestes to L. G. Monroe 11-1-1870 (11-3-1870)
Bull, E. A. to Jas. Harvey 6-3-1864 (6-20-1864)
Bull, Levana to Jordan W. Creasey 12-22-1863 (12-24-1863)
Bull, Sarah E. to James Hunter 6-24-1869
Burger, E. J. to James H. Heard 10-30-1858 (10-31-1858)
Burn, Mary to John Hogin 7-4-1868 (7-5-1868)
Butler, Elizabeth to C. W. Horner 4-6-1858
Butler?, Frances to B. F. Goodrich 8-7-1858 (8-12-1858)
Byler, Rena to Jno. Hammond 8-28-1863
Cagle, Margaret L. T. to Thos. T. Bone 1-13-1859
Campbell, Mary E. to Joseph Means 12-6-1869 (12-7-1869)
Carney, Susan Ann to Alfred C. Henley 12-26-1868 (12-27-1868)

Carr, Eliza to H. G. Austin 11-25-1857
Carr, Harriett P. to John J. Sellars 11-20-1865 (11-23-1865)
Carr, Mary J. to Alex Carr 8-3-1864 (8-5-1864)
Carr, Susan to J. M. Hall 3-10-1858
Carrell, Sarah J. to H. W. Williams 11-10-1866 (11-12-1866)
Carrington, Susan to E. J. Tatom 9-8-1858 (9-9-1858)
Carroll, S. A. to J. F. Foster 18-6-1857
Carroll, Susan to Solomon Potter 9-1-1862
Cathey, Elizabeth to William Yates 8-10-1867 (8-11-1867)
Cathey, Margaret to Thomas M. Davidson 7-14-1866 (7-15-1866)
Cathey, Susan to M. V. Adcock no date (with Oct 1866)
Cathy, Susan to M. V. Adcock 10-25-1866 (10-28-1866)
Cayce, M. C. to J. M. Bowers 11-1-1865 (11-13-1865)
Chadowin, Caroline to Benjamin F. Jones 7-22-1869 (7-26?-1869)
Chadwick, Emeline to Theophilus Woodward 9-3-1868
Chambers, Sarah to Austin Cook 4-30-1858
Chapel, M. E. to John Daughterty 4-14-1865
Chaudoin, Nancy J. to J. T. Jenkins 1-19-1864 (1-20-1864)
Chaudoin, Rebecca to Wiley Smothers 1-13-1864 (1-14-1864)
Chester, E. G. A. to J. C. R. Kelly 1-8-1869 (1-10-1869)
Chester, Sarah to G. W. McCloud 10-3-1868 (10-4-1868)
Choate, Brunette to T. B. McLyea 3-13-1865 (3-15-1865)
Choate, Ellen C. to Henderson Tilly 7-28-1858
Choate, Lucretia to Edward Matlock 8-16-1861
Choate, Lucretia C. to J. G. Williams 12-16-1865
Choate, Nellie to Bartley Moore 10-8-1857 (10-10-1857)
Christie, Mary A. to Michael Black 10-6-1858 (10-7-1858)
Clardy, C. T. to Wm. T. Luther 8-10-1864
Clardy, S. E. to T. C. Spears 10-13-1860 (10-14-1860)
Clifton, E. C. to W. J. Myatt 11-21-1864 (11-27-1864)
Climer, A. O. to Th. W. Underwood 6-13-1857 (6-14-1858?)
Climer, L. F. to M. A. Halliburton 10-3-1857 (10-5-1857)
Climer, Nancy to Jas. Chapel 4-14-1865 (4-30-1865)
Cocke, M. J. to R. G. Turner 9-16-1863
Cockmen, Mary A. to Levi V. Walker 12-27-1857 (12-30-1857)
Coleman, Aneliza E. to James W. Green 1-17-1870 (1-25-1870)
Coleman, Elizabeth to W. H. Napier 11-21-1857 (11-22-1857)
Coleman, Isabella to George W. Alsbrooks 4-25-1870
Conaly, Mary to Thos. Folay 9-24-1860
Cook, Sarah to Thomas J. Akin 10-4-1865
Cooksey, Cora to S.? M. Dotson 6-25-1867 (6-27-1867)
Cooksey, Sarah L. to Samuel J.? Allen 5-25-1867 (5-26-1867)
Cooley, Mary to Oatis Story 3-12-1859 (3-13-1859)
Cooley, R. C. to Wm. Bush 8-7-1864 (8-8-1864)
Coon, Rebecca F. to J. B. Byres 1-25-1860 (1-29-1860)
Corlew, Lucinda to Richd. D. Eubank 12-18-1860
Corlew, Malviny to T. L. Nicks 2-13-1867
Corlew, Pheba A. to B. R. Williams 9-23-1857
Corlew, S. F. to E. J. Harris 3-5-1857
Corlew, Sarah to George Long 12-15-1866 (12-16-1866)

Corlew, Sarah to George Long no date (with Dec 1866)
Corliew, E. F. to J. H. Larkins 9-4-1866 (9-5-1866)
Craft, C. E. to William A. Thompson 5-11-1867
Craft, Levica to Beverly Bruce 7-7-1858 (7-13-1858)
Craigh, Bettey Ann to Mackallen Balthrop 10-30-1869 (10-31-1869)
Crane, Mary Ann to William A. Sinks 5-10-1867 (5-12-1867)
Crane, S. F. to F. M. Climer 8-28-1857
Crawford, Calley to Makins? Murrell 12-21-1867 (12-24-1867)
Crawford, Louisa D. to A. J. Gunn 12-27-1868 (12-31-1868)
Creech, Elizabeth to Webb S. Taylor 11-30-1869 (12-5-1869)
Crockett, Emily to Samuel Runnols 11-13-1866 (11-14-1866)
Crockett, Mary C. to M. V. Reynolds 2-27-1858
Crow, Louisa to B. C. Potts 5-5-1864
Crow, Rachael M. to Elijah Daverson 2-21-1867
Cruise, Elizabeth to Albert Hunter 2-5-1860
Cullum, Martha T. to Jesse P. Cullum 5-1-1869 (5-3-1869)
Cunningham, M. E. to W. W. Carroll 8-10-1864
Cunningham, M. J. to Tho. M. W. Freeman 5-29-1861 (5-30-1861)
Cunningham, Sallie to Wm. Griffin 10-20-1863
Cunningham, Sarah E. to R. M. Carroll 2-6-1858 (2-7-1858)
Curtis, Sarah to W. J. Hays 12-28-1861 (12-29-1861)
Dailey, Sarah J. to P. A. Miller 11-24-1859 (11-27-1859)
Daniel, Bettie G. to A. J. Smith 2-3-1869
Daniel, Mary P. to Jos. Daniel 11-18-1861
Daniel, Susan F. to Tho. Spicer 10-8-1862 (10-9-1862)
Daniel, Tennessee D. to W. M. Adams 1-11-1866 (1-15-1866)
Davidson, Amanda to Jas. Booker 12-27-1864 (12-28-1864)
Davidson, E. A. to Charley Robinson 3-29-1858 (3-30-1858)
Davidson, Elizabeth to R. A. Johnson 9-3-1859 (9-4-1859)
Davidson, M. A. to F. P. Johnson 10-17-1864 (not certified)
Davidson, Nancy to Jno. M. Luther 9-24-1862 (10-1-1862)
Davidson, Sarah to S. W. Cathey 4-22-1864 (5-5-1864)
Davidson, Sarah A. to S. W. Cathey 12-28-1865
Davidson, Sarah Ann to Henry N. Johnson 1-25-1866 (1-28-1866)
Dawson, Elizer to H. H. Henderson 2-7-1866
Dawson, Nancy to John R. James 11-27-1865
Deasant, Manervy E. to Walter S. Winfrey 2-16-1866 (3-4-1866)
Deen, Frank? E. to Thos. J. Blount 5-16-1861
Deen, Parthena F. to Henry A. Bateman 3-28-1866
Dickson, Angie to W. M. Organ 11-29-1859
Dickson, M. E. to James T. Swift 4-11-1859
Dickson, P. D. to Wm. H. Dickson 12-27-1866
Dickson, S. W. to David A. Mitchell 1-18-1869 (1-20-1869)
Dickson, Sarah A. to W. C. Allen 12-28-1866 (1-1-1867)
Dickson, Tennessee A. to C. J. Martin 1-1-1867 (12?-1-1866)
Dillaha, Tennessee J. to J. M. Russell 11-25-1868 (11-26-1868)
Dilleha, Mary M. to George R. Moore 4-17-1869 (4-18-1869)
Dillehay, Susan A. to Joel N. Boaz 2-4-1859
Dodson, Dolly H. to W. D. Eleazer 1-30-1867
Dodson, Martha S. to Robert H. McClelland 5-26-1868 (5-27-1868)

Dodson, Nancy A. to John B. Grymes 11-11-1858
Dodson, Rebecca Ann to James Edwards 12-1-1869 (12-2-1869)
Dodson, S. A. to Jacob Hopper 9-15-1864
Dodson, Sarah E. to James H. Long 4-23-1868
Dodson, Sarah J. to William J. Loggins 1-20-1869 (1-21-1869)
Dodson, Susan to James S. England 2-5-1869 (2-6-1869)
Dotson, Clementine to William Lomax 7-27-1860 (8-2-1860)
Dotson, Margaret to Joseph Tummons 3-29-1866
Doty, Martha C. to Latham? G. Baker 12-20-1870
Dowden, Sarah to Joseph Lawrence 3-2-1870
Dudley, Amanda L. to John C. Dunnagan 3-4-1868 (3-5-1868)
Dudley, Tennesse ann to J. K. Clifton 7-31-1865 (8-3-1865)
Dugger, Arminta E. to Isaac Reed 5-24-1870
Dugger, Eliza to John T. Lufman 9-17-1870
Dugger, Mary to Geo. Etheridge 5-20-1857 (5-21-1857)
Duke, Mary to James Choat 12-17-1870 (12-18-1870)
Dunn, Annette to Wm. H. Hughes 5-31-1867
Dunn, Nancy J. to J. B. Rogers 7-9-1863
Dunnagan, A. J. to L. M. Craft 8-12-1863
Dunnagan, Arminta to Corder T. Weems 10-25-1869
Dunnagan, Josephine to W. H. Smith 8-6-1870 (8-7-1870)
Dunnagan, Louisa E. to George Brazzell 1-20-1866 (1-21-1866)
Dunnagan, Louisa P. to S. P. Larkins 7-18-1866 (7-19-1866)
Dunnagan, M. A. to G. H. Petty 11-28-1866
Dunnagan, Malona to John Blackburn 2-15-1858 (2-23-1858)
Dunnagan, Martha A. to Jacob Chadwick 12-21-1867 (12-22-1867)
Dunnagan, Mary A. to Eli T. Curtis 9-12-1857 9-13-1857)
Dunnagan, S. E. to M. V. Loftis 7-26-1859 (7-28-1859)
Dunnagan, Sarah J. to John W. Tucker 7-18-1860 (7-22-1860)
Dunnagan, Susan to W. H. Green 2-9-1870
Dunnaway, C. L. to John J. Henderson 6-14-1859
Dunnaway, E. A. to W. A. Shaw 1-26-1858
Edwards, Arminday Jane to W. T. Waller 4-15-1870 (4-19-1870)
Edwards, Elizabeth D. to Jno. T. Grove 4-7-1862
Edwards, Malinda to Henry Taylor 8-8-1866 (8-12-1866)
Edwards, Margaret to Melvin W. Story 11-11-1867
Edwards, S. E. to N. B. Harris 1-2-1865 (1-3-1865)
Edwards, Sarah to Geo. O. B. Mitchell 3-24-1860 (3-25-1860)
Elliott, Allice to William Beasley 5-28-1866 (5-29-1866)
England, Gemima A. to Jones D. Martin 3-29-1858 (3-30-1858)
England, M. D. to J. F. Choat 10-23-1869 (10-24-1869)
England, Mary E. to G. S. Rosser 9-7-1867 (9-11-1867)
England, Mary J. to Joseph Choat 12-22-1868
England, Mattilda M to J. D. Martin 12-17-1868 (12-20-1868)
England, Rebeca J. to M. H. Vinyard 8-21-1866 (8-30-1866)
England, Retly? to Joseph Williams 9-17-1866
England, Sarah E. to John T. May 12-3-1868
Ennis, Susan E. to D. F. Hudson 8-3-1863
Errington, Margaret to James F. Myatt 11-3-1866 (11-8-1866)
Estes, Lucy A. to Charles W. Warwick 2-23?-1868

Ethilliams, Ann to Thos. Tinley 12-28-1860 (1-1-1861)
Evans, Mary to Thomas England 3-2-1867
Evans, Sarah O. to Jos. T. Springer 1-19-1857 (1-20-1857)
Ferrel, Malvina to Martin Hampton 12-7-1866 (12-9-1866)
Ferrel, Melvina E. to Henry Underwood 3-8-1862 (3-6?-1862)
Ferrell, Laura N. to William Davidson 4-6-1869 (4-7-1869
Ferrell, sMary to Shelby Potter 5-26-1870 (5-31-1870)
Few, Adline to A. C. Dunnagan 2-6-1867
Few, M. L. to Joel jr. Erington 12-25-1866 (12-30-1866)
Few, Matilda to G. W. Evans 11-12-1862 (11-20-1862)
Finch, E. A. to W. B. Hassell 9-18-1861 (1-26-1862)
Finch, E. J. to G. W. Baker 12-26-1866 (1-2-1867)
Finch, M. E. to S. M. Elliott 4-8-1865 (4-10-1865)
Ford, P. A. to Jos. Taylor 3-19-1861 (3-20-1861)
Ford, Sarah Elizabeth to James White 4-17-1867
Foster, D. A. to A. H. Bone 1-15-1867
Foster, L. J. to James Finnie? 10-17-1862 (10-19-1862)
Foster, Sallie to James Jarmon 6-30-1860 (7-1-1860)
Fowler, Eliza A. to L. S. Nichol 11-20-1869 (11-21-1869)
Fowler, Mary Jane to James Fowler 9-9-1865 (9-10-1865)
Fowlkes, Martha Ellen to George Fletcher 6-4-1870 (6-5-1870)
Fox, Janie to W. M. Kinser 9-5-1870 (9-6-1870)
Frasher, E. A. to W. N. Edney 3-22-1861 (3-24-1861)
Frasher, Sarah E. to Pleasant Frasher 8-17-1866 (8-19-1866)
Freeman, Rebecca A. to J. T. Harvy 1-5-1867 (1-14-1867)
Frost, Elizabeth to Jno. M. Bruce 3-20-1860 (3-21-1860)
Fussell, M. J. to John J. Sanders 12-30-1869
Fussell, Missouri to J. W. Adcock 1-31-1867
Gadby, Fannie to J. B. Dobson 3-25-1861
Gamble, C. E. to W. P. Robbins 8-17-1861
Garland, Lucinda to John Charuthers 4-18-1870 (4-19-1870)
Garrett (Gossett?), Sarah J. to Parson Jackson 12-11-1867 (12-17-1867)
Garton, Clara to John J. Sellars 10-13-1859 (10-2?-1859)
Garton, Elizabeth to Daniel Parker 10-25-1864 (10-18?-1864)
Garton, Harriet M. to Jackson Rawls 8-8-1862
Garton, Huldy to John Dilyard 1-4-1866 (1-3?-1866)
Garton, Louisiana to B. F. Brown 9-19-1862 (9-20-1862)
Garton, Lucinda to S. M. Tidwell 2-5-1867 (2-7-1867)
Garton, Susan to John Welch 8-12-1867 (8-14-1867)
Garton, Tennessee to O. C. Spicer 11-16-1861 (11-17-1861)
Garton, Tessa to H. C. Thomas 2-17-1858
Gentry, Martha J. to M. H. Meek 2-25-1862
Gentry, Mary to James D. Austin 3-25-1857
Gilbert, Indiana to David R. Williams 2-14-1860
Gillan, Mary to Ed Williams 4-29-1865 (4-30-1865)
Gilland, Kanzadie to James Adams 3-21-1866 (3-22-1866)
Gilland, Mary to James Lappay? 1-6-1866 (1-7-1866)
Gillin, Elizabeth to G. M. Mulky 8-8-1864 (8-11-1864)
Gillmore, M. A. to Geo. M. Dickson 10-17-1864 (10-20-1864)
Gilmore, Lucy B. to W. P. Sensing 11-28-1861

Gilmore, Mary M. to David Robertson 7-30-1868
Gilmore, N.? C. to M. Taylor 1-30-1864
Gilmore, Sarah J. to Geo. Ragain 10-20-1863 (10-22-1863)
Gilmore, Tennie to W. W. Roberson 9-16-1867 (9-17-1867)
Givens, M. F. to J. N. Lewis 1-24-1863 (1-28-1863)
Glasgow, Jack Ann to Samuel Coalman 2-23-1870 (2-24-1870)
Glass, Jane to John Sears 8-8-1868 (8-9-1868)
Glassgo, Matilda to John Taylor 1-17-1857
Godfrey, Jane to J. O. Patey 9-1-1870
Godwin, Martha T. to H. W. Fulks 2-25-1870 (2-21?-1870)
Gold, Florance to A. G. jr. Goodlet 6-8-1866 (6-10-1866)
Goodin, M. A. to Henry Denny 6-6-1864
Goodrich, Jeniatta J. to Isaac? McLaughlin 9-10-1859 (9-13-1859)
Goodrich, Sophia to W. M. Yeates 11-25-1857 (12-8-1857)
Goodrich, Susan to James Brazzell 10-31-1863 (10-7?-1863)
Goodwin, Elizabeth to Wm. Etheridge 7-18-1860
Gordon, Malissa A. to B. W. Cunningham 7-7-1857 (7-12-1857)
Gossett (Garrett?), R. Jane to W. D. Chappell 3-29-1858 (4-1-1858)
Gower, Nancy J. to Jas. Anderson 12-30-1862 (12-31-1862)
Graham, Sarah M. to V. S. Loftis 12-11-1865
Gray, H.? M.? to John? Haney 9-15-1870
Gray, Lucy to W. E. Watkin 8-3-1863 (8-6-1863)
Gray, Martha to Robert Hamilton 9-30-1865 (10-1-1865)
Gray, Martha V. to Charles Miller 7-25-1865 (7-26-1865)
Gray, Sarah E. to William H. Guinn 2-18-1868 (2-19-1868)
Green, C. to Geo. Marlow 10-13-1860 (10-14-1860)
Green, S. A. to J. R. Slayden 1-18-1863 (1-19-1863)
Greer, Ann to J. K. Brown 12-29-1857
Greer, E. T. (Mrs.) to James Yates 3-28-1862 (3-30-1862)
Gregory, Jane to Saml? Sills 2-14-1861
Grigsby, S. C. to D. S. Majors 5-29-1867
Grove, Mary Jane to Franklin Dillard 3-31-1866 (4-1-1866)
Grymes, Mary J. to Wm. James Long 6-12-1860
Guinn, Nancy to Wm. Cowen 4-14-1858 (4-15-1858)
Gust?, Susan C. to Richard C. True 12-7-1860
Hagwood, Fredonia to A. J. Williams 5-12-1868
Hainy, L. to John Brock 2-14-1857 (2-15-1857)
Hale, Martha S. to J. G. Sweny 12-14-1858 (12-15-1858)
Hale, Nancy C. to James P. Lovell 1-24-1867
Haley, Mary K. to Thos. B. Yates 2-24-1865 (2-26-1865)
Haley, Nancy to James Haley 3-13-1860 (3-15-1860)
Hall, Anelizer to Dempsey Summer 12-1-1866 (12-2-1866)
Hall, Dealatha J. to Joseph Edwards 2-18-1868 (2-20-1868)
Hall, M. M. to John Oconell 2-25-1860 (2-26-1860)
Hall, Martha E. to G. P. Y. Epps 3-14-1866
Hall, Mary A. to John A. Jones 1-30-1860 (2-8-1860)
Hall, Mary S. to John Q. Taylor 1-26-1867 (1-27-1867)
Hall, Nancy to John N. Hood 1-2-1869 (1-3-1869)
Hall, P. E. to Geo. W. Hill 9-3-1861
Hall, Sallie M. to J. R. Stewart 11-12-1868

Hambrick, Amandey to David A. Campbell 1-12-1863
Hampton, S. C. to Robert Patterson 5-28-1870 (5-29-1870)
Haney, Mary L. to John H. Thomas 5-4-1866
Hanks, Lucy E. to M. Howard 9-18-1857 (9-20-1857)
Harbison, Lee A. to A. J. Nesbett 12-26-1857 (12-27-1857)
Hardin, F. B. to Hamilton Parks 11-13-1869 (11-14-1869)
Harley, Mattilda J. to J. R. B. Hayse 12-26-1868 (12-27-1868)
Harper, Hannah M. to Samuel Patterson 11-11-1870
Harper, Henrietta A. to Augustin Nicks 10-18-1870
Harrell, Elizabeth R. to Henry Picket 4-13-1869 (4-14-1869)
Harrell, Nancy C. to James J. England 12-22-1860 (12-24-1860)
Harris, Fredonia to James P. Gentry 3-21-1866
Harris, G. A. to A. B. Sensing 3-6-1867
Harris, Mary J. to Mathew L. Gentry 1-9-1860 (1-10-1860)
Harris, Mary T. to Galvin McLaughlin 9-24-1859 (9-28-1859)
Harris, Nannie F. to J. C. Harris 12-18-1865 (12-21-1865)
Harris, Sarah to Wm. Bensinger 2-2-1864 (2-11-1864)
Harris, Sarah C. to John H. Hodges 2-10-1859
Harris, Sarah ann to J. B. Williams 8-24-1865
Hartigan, Bettie N. to A. J. H. Crown 8-31-1859 (9-1-1859)
Harvey, Eliza A. to J. F. Davis 12-31-1869 (1-5-1870)
Harvey, Martha A. to D. R. Hickerson 8-14-1858 (8-15-1858)
Haskins, Susan to James M. Bryant 9-11-1870
Hatley, Elizabeth to Ben A. Jackson 7-15-1858
Hatley, Mallinda to C. G. H. Rose 7-31-1869
Hatley, Polly to J. L. Felts 3-18-1861 (3-19-1861)
Hay, C. to J. B. Baird 1-2-1864 (1-3-1864)
Hay, Keziah to D. H. Lankford 6-14-1865 (6-15-1865)
Hays, Elizabeth E. to John E. Sensing 6-20-1859
Hays, Rutha A. C. to Jacob Seals 8-30-1857
Hays, S. J. to G. W. L. Lewis 3-28-1859 (3-31-1859)
Heard, Mary to William R. Roberts 7-20-1867 (7-31-1867)
Heath, Eliza to S. M. Crow 7-12-1870
Heath, Elizabeth Jane to James Adams 11-26-1866
Heath, Margaret to Frank Evans 5-9-1864
Heath, Susan E. to Wm. H. Sestler 9-15-1865 (11-14-1865)
Hedge, Mary A. to John R. Gunn 1-3-1861 (1-6-1861)
Heggie, Nannie M. to R. Searcy 2-20-1862 (4-2-1862)
Hegwood, Elizabeth to William O. Kain 12-24-1866 (12-26-1866)
Hegwood, Martha Ann to Wm. H. Linsey 3-5-1866 (3-6-1866)
Hendrick, Sarah to Wm. M. Kirk 12-25-1860
Henley, E. A. to Wm. Bryant 4-3-1860 (4-4-1860)
Henley, Jane to Thomas Lyles 9-23-1862
Henton, Rachael A. to Rufus J. Goostree 9-7-1868 (9-8-1868)
Herberson, Clary E. to Samuel Hammon 9-24-1866 (10-17-1866)
Herbison, Julia F. to George M. Puett 10-24-1867 (10-27-1867)
Herrin, Agnes to Franklin Jones 5-6-1867 (5-9-1867)
Hibbs, Frances to Wm. Duncan 2-12-1864
Hibbs, Frances to W. B. Tatom 9-10-1866 (9-11-1866)
Hibbs, V. L. M. to R. M. Campbell 5-30-1864 (5-31-1864)

Hickerson, Mary F. to Oney S. Harvey 6-16-1866 (6-24-1866)
Hickerson, S. L. to Jack Harvey 4-3-1858 (4-4-1858)
Hiland, Ann J. to James E. Justice 10-8-1859 (10-12-1859)
Hill, Geo. Ann to G. M. Decker 3-10-1858
Hodges, Martha E. to W. S. Weakley 3-3-1858
Hogan, C. C. to William Keys 7-19-1870 (7-21-1870)
Holland, M. J. to Jas. P. Hedge 12-22-1864
Holt, Ellen D. to S. J. A. Wells 4-26-1858
Hood, E. A. to Britton Johnson 4-9-1859 (3-10-1859?)
Hood, Mary A. to Joshua Cathey 6-23-1857 (6-24-1857)
Hooper, Elizabeth to Thos. B. Larkins 11-25-1861 (11-26-1861)
Hooper, Franky H. to Jno. J. Larkins 8-14-1858 (8-15-1858)
Hooper, Jane to J. J. Price 11-16-1867 (11-20-1868?)
Hopely, Pauline L. to A. W. Wilber 12-23-1865 (12-24-1865)
Hopper, Nancy M. to Joseph M. Green 8-11-1865
Horner, Mary O. to Spencer A. Myatt 12-19-1866 (12-20-1866)
Howel, Ruth to Reuben Price 1-10-1865 (1-11-1865)
Howell, E. R. to Hiram Bryles 7-28-1862
Howell, Elizabeth to J. W. Daugherty 5-24-1858 (5-27-1858)
Hudgins, E. A. to N. P.? Nicks 3-22-1863
Hudson, Amanda to W. J. W. J. Berry 11-20-1869 (11-21-1869)
Hudson, Laurentine to Benj. F. Baker 10-20-1866
Hughes, Mary A. to Henderson Corlew 12-21-1859 (12-22-1859)
Hughes, Mary V. to William Davidson 12-25-1866
Humphreys, Gemima to John Rye 6-12-1858 (6-13-1858)
Hunter, Elizabeth to Nicholas Shufield? 1-16-1861 (1-20-1861)
Hunter, Jack Ann to C. M. Glasgow 10-15-1862 (10-16-1862)
Hunter, Louisa to William M. Mitchell 10-14-1867 (10-16-1867)
Hunter, Louisa J. to Thos. S. Young 12-25-1858 (12-26-1858)
Hunter, Martha to William Brumit 9-30-1870
Hunter, Martha G. to J. M. Glassgo 10-21-1858
Hunter, Mary A. to Jas. M. Smith 3-16-1864 (3-17-1864)
Hunter, Mary F. to J. M. Glasgow 12-3-1869 (12-5-1869)
Hunter, Minerva to John Lindsey 5-13-1868
Hunter, Parlee J. to William C. Scott 9-4-1869 (9-2?-1869)
Hunter, Rebecca to Wash Mitchell 12-18-1860 (12-23-1860)
Hutchison, L. to Wm. Lankford 8-13-1859 (8-22-1859)
Hutson, L. C. to Blount Baker 9-7-1860 (9-20-1860)
Hutson, Nancy J. to Thomas J. James 11-21-1870 (11-24-1870)
Jackson, Amanda to Lawrence Bellfield 12-25-1866 (12-28-1866)
Jackson, Araminta to J. C. Dotson 2-3-1858
Jackson, D. A. to C. C. Jackson 4-13-1863
Jackson, E. C. to John N. Hood 9-1-1857
Jackson, Louisa J. to M. M. Hiland 11-26-1869
Jackson, Malvina to John H. Baker 2-16-1870
Jackson, Martha J. to E. D. Monroe 8-14-1862 (8-16-1862)
Jackson, Mary E. to William Hagwood 3-28-1867
Jackson, Sarah M. to Robert B. Stone 1-21-1868 (1-22-1868)
Jackson, Susan to E. Heath 11-13-1861
Jackson, Tennessee to Thomas Sesler 7-7-1862 (7-15-1862)

James, Araminnta M. to James L. Bybee 9-8-1866
James, E. C. to A. C. Parrish 1-16-1865 (1-17-1865)
James, Sarah L. (C.?) to W. J. Craig 3-12-1858 (3-14-1858)
James, Susan C. to William Johnson 12-23-1867 (12-24-1867)
James, Susan J. to W. H. Harley 1-24-1857 (1-25-1857)
Jarman, Sarah C. to Thos. Lile 7-2-1864
Jarnagan, S. H. to J. B. Henson 9-11-1867
Jarnigan, Susan S. to J. G. jr. Hinson 2-26-1862 (2-27-1862)
Johnson, Mallinda to Levi G. Fry 10-12-1869 (11-10-1869)
Johnson, Martha A. to Robert A. Duke 10-8-1859 (10-13-1859)
Johnson, Sarah E. to A. J. Yates 6-30-1866 (7-5-1866)
Johnston, Sarah J. to S. A. Tidwell 7-20-1870
Johnston, Susanah C. to James L. Parker 7-18-1867 (7-7?-1867)
Jones, A. A. to G. C. Williams 8-31-1870 (9-1-1870)
Jones, Allice P. to Wilson Capps 11-9-1865
Jones, Amanda to F. M. Sampson 10-5-1869 (10-6-1869)
Jones, Elizabeth to R. Chadoin 12-1-1860 (12-3-1860)
Jones, Ellen A. to John H. Burrows? 1-19-1864 (1-24-1864)
Jones, F. C. to M. Cooley 8-22-1864
Jones, Martha W. to Milton B. Patten 10-12-1859 (10-13-1859)
Jones, Mary to Thomas Whitfield 3-7-1867 (3-10-1867)
Jones, Mary A. to George P. Deal 7-28-1866 (7-30-1866)
Jones, Nancy Ann to P T. Seals 5-26-1870
Jones, S. E. A. to J. E. Averett 10-16-1867
Jones, Tennessee to Wm. T. Nisson 6-24-1870 (6-26-1870)
Joslin, Elizabeth to John Caufman 2-?-1858 (2-10-1858)
Joslin, Elizabeth to John Young 11-18-1869
Joslin, Harriet to Webb? Nicks 12-24-1859 (12-29-1859)
Joslin, Louisa C. to J. W. Gill 8-8-1865 (8-10-1865)
Joslin, Martha to Washington Hunter 6-15-1867
Joslin, Nelly to Benj. Creech 11-23-1864 (11-27-1864)
Kain, Isabella to Warner Hodge 12-22-1870 (12-23-1870)
Karns, Mary Ann to Epps J. Thompson 9-21-1859 (9-22-1859)
Kee, Fredonia to James J. Hughes 12-22-1870
Kellum, Olive J. to J. M. Stokes 1-20-1868 (1-21-1868)
Kellum, Susan to E. E. Capps 7-29-1863
Kenedy, M. C. to G. W. Swift 12-23-1867 (12-24-1867)
Kephart, Nancy D. to W. J. Gafford 12-27-1865
Kephart, Penina to Leroy R. Lindsey 12-28-1859 (1-8-1860)
King, Eddy to Geo. Loftis 2-21-1862 (2-23-1862)
Kinzer, Charlott B. to John F. McWilliams 3-11-1870
Kirk, M.J. to W. T. Tucker 6-1-1857 (6-2-1857)
Kye, Julia P. to F. McCaslin 6-1-1863 (6-18-1863)
Ladd, Martha to Wm. Luther 12-15-1864
Ladd, Mary to John Brown 7-21-1865 (7-23-1865)
Ladd, Rebecca to Jackson Brown 12-12-1860
Ladd, Tennessee A. to G. L. Grove 10-10-1867
Lamastus, M. C. to L. S. Bond 2-29-1864
Lampley, Emiline to J. H. Hall 12-18-1864 (12-19-1864)
Lampley, M. A. to A. S. Griffin 2-28-1865 (3-1-1865)

Lampley, Martha to Wilson Tidwell 2-4-1860 (2-12-1860)
Lampley, Nancy to John Brown 2-2-1864 (2-7-1864)
Lampley, Tennessee to James Buttrey 11-26-1868 (12-17-1868)
Langford, Louisa P. to W. T. Weems 1-31-1866
Lankford, Louisa M. to W. L. Weemes 1-17-1867
Lankford, Mary to Jos.? Parker 1-2-1860 (1-5-1860)
Larkins, Amanda E. to William T. Overton 1-26-1867 (1-27-1867)
Larkins, J. W. to P. F. Leech 3-26-1861
Larkins, Lucy Jane to Matt Anderson 12-23-1869
Larkins, M. J. to J. A. Hendrick 7-31-1870
Larkins, Mary C. to John A. Dunlap 1-3-1865
Larkins, Mary Jane to A. C. Stockard 11-2-1865
Larkins, R. A. to J. S. Daniel 7-28-1864
Larkins, Sarah E. to William J. Mathis 9-10-1868
Latham, G. A. P. to Jas. H. Sullivan 1-16-1865 (1-18-1865)
Lavis?, C. O. to B. C. White? 3-14-1863
Lawrence, Nacy R. to John Lona 3-31-1863 (4-2-1863)
Lawson, Mary M. to John Coyne 3-29-1860 (6-18-1860)
Lea, Nancy A. J. to John H. Weaver 9-7-1868 (9-10-1868)
Leathers, Catherine to Dennis Bruce 10-5-1863 (10-8-1863)
Leathers, Kisiah to Silas Bruce 9-22-1857
Lee, Victoria to John W. Mitchel 9-25-1867 (9-26-1867)
Legget, Sarah to Jas. Hase 9-1-1864 (9-4-1864)
Lewallen, M. A. F. to Morris R. Cathey 8-23-1859 (8-24-1859)
Lewis, Mary A. to E. C. Cooley 7-8-1858 (7-10-1858)
Link, Mary E. to John A. Hampton 2-21-1868 (2-28-1868)
Linzey, A. J. to Thomas B. Harris 8-2-1869 (8-3-1869)
Linzey, Frances to John Creach 3-7-1870 (3-8-1870)
Linzey, Louisa to J. M. Gafford 5-2-1868
Linzey, Missouria to J. P. Gafford 7-10-1866 (7-13-1866)
Littrel, S. M. to W. T. Collins 3-4-1859 (3-10-1859)
Lloyd, M. J. to James Thomason 5-4-1857 (5-10-1857)
Loftis, Clara to Anthony F. Dudley 12-7-1859 (12-8-1859)
Loftis, Sarah to James Trammel 1-5-1857 (1-19-1857)
Loggins, M. A. to Geo. W. Daniel 12-12-1864 (12-29-1864)
Loggins, Mary to J. C. Daniel 10-7-1857
Long, Elizabeth to Alford Laine 10-17-1858
Long, Nancy J. to O. D. Caldwell 1-5-1867 (1-6-1867)
Lowe, Laura A. to P. P. Neblett 6-29-1857 (6-30-1857)
Luther, Mary A. to W. H. Ladd 9-30-1862
Luther, Mary A. to Thomas S. Register 10-31-1868
Luther, Sarah to William C. Hall 1-13-1870
Luttrell, Sarah to E. D. Osbourn 1-15?-1868
Manley, S. C. to J. J. Higgins 5-11-1868
Marsh, M. E. to S. H. Petty 1-27-1864 (1-28-1864)
Marsh, Margaret E. to John N. H. Lankford 5-10-1861
Marsh, Mary J. to Jos. L. Mills 11-29-1862
Marsh?, Mary J. to Martin Clancy 9-28-1860 (9-29-1860)
Martin, Geo. Ann to R. L. England 9-18-1858 (9-19-1858)
Martin, J. E. to W. J. Hagey 9-24-1870 (9-25-1870)

Martin, Margaret A. to Wm. H. Brown 11-19-1866
Martin, Mary C. to Eli Perry 7-16-1870 (7-17-1870)
Martin, Mary E. to James R. Brazzell 7-17-1858 (7-18-1858)
Martin, Nancy C. to G. D. V. Schmittou 1-31-1857 (2-3-1857)
Martin, Sallie A. to James R. Brazzell 1-18-1869 (1-19-1869)
Mathews, Ann J. to W. H. Binkley 1-6-1862 (1-9-1862)
Mathews, Jennie to J. N. Williams 2-4-1864
Mathews, Martha to Noah Stewart 6-9-1857 (6-11-1857)
Mathews, Nancy Ann to G. W. Toler 7-6-1867
Mathis, A. M. to J. M. Mathis 10-17-1860 (10-21-1860)
Mathis, Betsey J. to P. H. Adams 1-24-1862
Mathis, Elizabeth to William H. Smith 6-29-1868 (7-1-1868)
Mathis, Elizer to S. C. Runyan 1-11-1866 (1-21-1866)
Mathis, Martha to Philip H. Deason 9-14-1865
Mathis, Martha to Jno. C. Stewart 8-25-1858 (8-28-1858)
Mathis, Mary to Andrew Wallace 7-28-1857
Mathis, Mary L. to Stephen Adams 8-27-1868 (8-31-1868)
Mathis, Matilda to C. T. Mixon 9-19-1864
Mathis, Sarah to E. H. Naramore 12-10-1859 (12-23-1859)
Mathis, Sarah Jane to Ancel Adams 5-19-1857 (5-19-1857)
Mathis, Willella F. to John V. Jackson 11-12-1868
Matlock, E. V. O. to A. N. Stroud 11-19-1870
Matlock, J. M. to R. B. Brown 6-6-1865
Matlock, Lucy A. to L. B. Cooley 9-26-1867
Matlock, Mahala T. to W. H. Jackson 9-29-1865
Matlock, Mary to J. C. R. Critchard 12-12-1863
Matlock, Sarah Ann to John W. Williams 8-20-1870 (8-21-1870)
Matthews, Jane to Joseph Allison 8-22-1868
May, Anna E. to W. J. Adams 2-26-1866 (2-27-1866)
Mayberry, Martha A. to John A. Weakley 10-6-1868 (10-3?-1868)
Mayberry, Sarah to Albert S. Mitchell 12-25-1867
Mayfield, Berdilla M. to Wm. Lee 6-18-1859 (6-19-1859)
Mayfield, Susan to Manley Hatley 2-3-1859
McCall, Emily to Wm. James Hudgens 1-12-1860
McCauley, Catharine to J. M. Talley 1-1-1868
McClelland, Angeline to J. K. Nichols 1-29-1870 (1-30-1870)
McClelland, Sarah to Wm. Mayberry 2-20-1858 (2-21-1858)
McCollum, Sarah to Robt. Steele 5-2-1861
McCormack, Mary Jane to James F. Williams 10-8-1870 (10-9-1870)
McCormick, L. A. to H. L. Duke 7-9-1870 (7-10-1870)
McCoy, M. C. to George Adcock 5-26-1870
McCrary, Huldah to J. A. Ledford 8-29-1864 (8-31-1864)
McCrary, M. E. to Jackson Hyde 8-18-1864 (8-22-1864)
McCrary, Meshia to Henry Davis 6-2-1868 (6-7-1868)
McCreary, Jane to Soloman Reep 4-12-1870 (4-19-1870)
McGaw, Nancy L. to John Lyles 7-10-1860 (7-11-1860)
McKechnie, Agness to John O. Ladd 2-13-1861 (2-14-1861)
McKelvy, Lucy to F. B. Orgorman 4-4-1865
McLaughlin, Nannie? A. to Thos. M. Hale 11-1-1859 (11-30-1859)
McMahan, Malita to Jas. S. Jackson 3-14-1865

McMahan, Mary J. to Henry W. Thompson 8-25-1869
McNeely, E. J. to James N. Allen 4-23-1863
McNeilley, Juley G. to James M. Allen 10-6-1870
McTagill, Bridget to Alexr. McKinstrey 4-11-1861
Meek, Comfort to Thos. B. Gentry 12-5-1863 (not executed)
Meek, Ferby to David G. Gentry 1-5-1867 (1-6-1867)
Michel, Arbella J. to James Hendrick 11-4-1867
Milam, Thankful J. to William N. Raymond 11-2-1867 (11-3-1867)
Miller, E. J. to W. B. Tatom 10-30-1858
Miller, Sallie to J. H. Bishop 5-25-1867 (5-26-1867)
Miller, Sarah to Madison Dunnagan 5-14-1870 (5-15-1870)
Mills, Sarah C. to James Mathews 1-2-1858 (1-4-1858)
Mitchel, Emily to Judge Jackson 3-21-1870
Mitchel, Martha to Henderson King 9-1-1866 (9-2-1866)
Mitchell, Jaldean? to Saml. F. Gilmore 11-19-1857 (11-20-1857)
Mixon, M. A. to A. Swift 8-19-1864 (8-20-1864)
Moore, Dicey M. to Frank Moss 8-27-1857 (8-28-1857)
Moore, Nancy to John I. J. Adams 3-11-1858
Morgan, Emily to C. H. Kiertner 2-23-1857 (2-12?-1857)
Morgan, Mary J. to Blount Harvey 1-12-1863 (1-15-1863)
Morris, Saphrona to R. B. Murphey 10-3-1857 (10-4-1857)
Morrison, Martha J. to James H. Parrish 5-12-1869 (5-13-1869)
Murphy, Arbella to Nicholas Baker 11-16-1868
Murrell, Eleanora to J. F. Martin 9-5-1867 (9-6-1867)
Murrell, N. J. to G. Adcock 6-3-1864 (6-5-1864)
Murrell, Polly Ann to Chas. Bird 10-20-1862 (10-22-1862)
Murrell, Rachael to Augustin Baker 1-11-1859 (1-12-1859)
Murrell, Sarah to Louis M. Franklin 8-24-1865
Murrell, Susan A. to Levi S. Petty 10-21-1861 (10-20?-1861)
Murrell, Susan R. to James Owens 5-28-1867 (5-29-1867)
Murrell?, Margaret to John McCoy 3-14-1857 (3-15-1857)
Musgroves, Darcus to Henderson Proctor 4-10-1858 (4-11-1858)
Myatt, C. to James Bruce 12-3-1863 (12-9-1863)
Myatt, Charity J. to John S. Petty 10-11-1870 (10-13-1870)
Myatt, F. H. to C. R. Yates 1-13-1865
Myatt, Mary J. to Isaac O. Yates 8-15-1868 (8-16-1868)
Myatt, N. E. to E. Y. Andrews 9-30-1864
Myatt, R. E. to S. H. Adcock 10-22-1870 (10-27-1870)
Myatt, Rebecca P. to William J. Simpson 11-?-1867
Naibers?, Elizabeth to J.? R.? Taylor 3-12-1863
Nalls, Mary A. to Wm. Taylor 6-29-1865
Nance, Mary E. to Stokley Elliott 4-7-1866 (4-8-1866)
Naramore, Sarah J. to Robt. M. Tipton 5-7-1864 (5-11-1864)
Nash, E. A. to E. J. Tidwell 1-17-1865
Nash, N. M. to W. W. England 2-4-1867 (2-8-1867)
Nash, S. J. to D. Manley 6-3-1864
Nelson, Susan C. to Carter Jeans 1-10-1862 (1-13-1862)
Nesbitt, Elizabeth A. to Henry C. Gunn 12-1-1866 (12-2-1866)
Nesbitt, Elizabeth D. to A. W. Wooten 8-28-1869 (10-5-1869)
Nesbitt, Mary J. to Benj. G. Clark 1-21-1858

Nesbitt, N. A. W. to W. N. M. Berry 11-26-1864 (12-6-1864)
Newman, Frances C. to J. D. Roberson 6-30-1866 (7-1?-1866)
Newmon, M. J. to D. G. Robertson 7-19-1864
Nicholl, A. M. F. to W. B. Tatom 4-7-1858 (4-8-1858)
Nichols, M. A. to W. H. Hunt 10-13-1863
Nick, S. L. to R. H. Rose 12-23-1863
Nicks, A. G. to E. C. Harper 9-22-1870
Nicks, I. J. to T. P. Blocker 1-19-1867 (1-20-1867)
Nicks, Martha E. to Benjamin T. McCaslin 12-20-1866
Nicks, Mary R. to John Huggins 3-7-1869
Nicks, Salena E. to John R. Hooper 8-21-1869 (8-22-1869)
Norris, F. E. to W. D. Morrisett 8-15-1857
Norris, Fredonia C. to Henry C. Smith 11-2-1869 (11-7-1869)
Norris, Missouri to J. C. Kamey 9-30-1865 (10-8-1865)
Noughton, Sarah to M. Ward 11-18-1861 (11-20-1861)
Oakley, Jennette M. to George S. Allen 3-18-1862
Oakley, Mary T. to John W. Richardson 2-10-1858 (2-13-1858)
Oliver, Malinda to J. F. Cloud 10-21-1863
Overton, Hula B. to R. M. Baldwin 8-9-1864 (8-10-1864)
Owens, Jemima to John A. J. Russell 7-4-1860
Owens, M. E. to C. M. Kapehart 5-14-1870
Owens, Mary to Martin Fisher 7-22-1864 (7-23-1864)
Owens, Susan to M. T. Fowler 7-28-1870 (7-31-1870)
Pack, Frances to William Russell 5-18-1860
Pamenter?, E. G. to J. H. Copley 12-28-1870
Parker, Caroline to Daniel White 11-4-1862
Parker, Harriet M. to L. D. J. Lankford 7-16-1860 (7-19-1860)
Parker, M. L. to Jos. Nesbitt 9-28-1863 (10-1-1863)
Parker, Rebecca H. to W. P. A. Frasher 6-20-1862
Parmenter, Virginia to R. F. Street 5-4-1868 (5-7-1868)
Parmer, Adline to Van T. Rose 9-6-1865
Parrish, Anna T. to William H. Rice 12-11-1867 (12-17-1867)
Parrish, R. A. to R. F. M. Craige 11-2-1864 (11-3-1864)
Parrott, Martha J. to James W. Foster 12-23-1859 (12-27-1859)
Paterson, Jemimah to G. J. Winick 8-5-1865 (8-7-1865)
Patey, Cora L. to John McClurkan 7-31-1857 (8-2-1857)
Patterson, Rebecca to J. H. Russell 1-27-1862 (1-29-1862)
Patterson, Susan to David Wallace 3-2-1857 (3-3-1857)
Paty, Elinora? F. to Samuel T. Walker 2-5-1867 (2-14-1867)
Paty, Ellenory to J. M. Roberson 2-8-1866
Pavatt, Mary T. to James M. Corlew 10-5-1870
Pavatt, R. J. to J. B. Cording 5-11-1859
Payne, H. B. to A. W. Ray 9-26-1863 (9-27-1863)
Payne, H. B. to John H. Sensing 12-27-1860
Pendergrass, Emily to James Smith 11-18-1870 (11-20-1870)
Pendergrass, Jemima to James Glass 8-6-1860
Pendergrass, Rebecca to W. R. Daniel 8-3-1858 (8-4-1858)
Pentecost, Victoria E. to Wiley M. Stokes 2-11-1868 (2-13-1868)
Perkins, L. to J. Patton 6-3-1864 (10-27-1864)
Perkins, Mary A. to W. B. Brim 7-8-1865 (7-9?-1865)

Pernell, Fanney to J. A. Price 4-25-1857
Perry, Harriet to Denny R. Williams 4-9-1866
Perry, Mary to Thomas E. Hall 7-18-1867 (7-21-1867)
Pettey, Tennessee to Benjamin Goodrich 2-29-1868 (3-1-1868)
Petty, Lucinda P. to James L. Gentry 5-15-1869 (5-16-1869)
Petty, Perlina to Jackson Petty 12-21-1868
Petty, Tennessee A. to Aaron B. Butler 12-26-1867 (12-22?-1867)
Philips, Delia to J. J. Priest 2-9-1867 (2-10-1867)
Phillipps, E. to W. F. Dunnagan 7-7-1859 (7-21-1859)
Phillips, Louisa to J. W. Lampley 12-27-1864 (12-31-1864)
Phillips, M. E. to A. R. Vinyard 9-18-1860
Phillips, Martha Ann to Z. M. Groves 12-28-1869
Phipps, Margaret to James B. Grymes 1-21-1863 (1-22-1863)
Pickett, E. R. to George Corey 7-27-1870 (7-30-1870)
Pickett, Mary to W. Turner 10-16-1865
Pickett, Mary Jane to C. D. White 1-26-1870 (1-27-1870)
Pickett, Mattie D. to Levi W. Erlinger 3-4-1867
Pinson, M. A.? to J.W. Hunter 12-3-1863 (12-6-1863)
Pinson, Mary M. to William B. Hunter 5-22-1869 (5-23-1869)
Pistol, Laminty to Brittain Yates 10-29-1860 (10-30-1860)
Porter, Mary E. to James M. Owens 12-13-1860
Porter, Mary Martha to Marion Rutlege 1-11-1866 (1-12-1866)
Porter, Susan to George R. Hooper 2-18-1869
Porter, Susan A. to Wm. Hill 4-16-1862
Porter, Tennessee C. to Thomas J. Carr 12-24-1867 (12-26-1867)
Porter, Virginia H. to J. M. Luther 6-5-1865 (6-8-1865)
Potter, Lucinda E. to E. T. Hassell 10-22-1859 (10-23-1859)
Potts, Amanda to S. B. Martin 9-10-1869 (9-15-1869)
Price, Ellen to James C. Gilleland 1-23-1867
Price, Martha J. to Gilbert Deloch 10-12-1870
Price, Rebecca to John Byars 8-8-1864 (8-9-1864)
Prichard, R. J. to R. B. Herbison 8-18-1863
Prichett, M. A. to W. M. White 11-16-1866 (11-26-1866)
Prockter, Harriet to J. W. Williams 9-8-1869 (9-10-1869)
Prockter, Margaret E. to H. B. Wall 11-2-1867 (11-3-1867)
Prockter, Missourea F. to F. M. Huggeans 1-5-1867 (1-6-1867)
Proctor, Bettie A. to John A. J. Reaves 11-8-1860
Proctor, E. V. to C. M. Carrall 2-2-1862 (2-3-1862)
Proctor, S. A. to S. Patterson 12-23-1858
Qualls, Ann to Uriah Smith 7-5-1864
Quarles, Mary to Robert Matlock 9-15-1869
Ragan, Jennetta to Richard H. Ballard 8-24-1857 (9-1-1857)
Ragan, M. E. to John J. Turner 9-7-1864 (9-8-1864)
Ragan, Maliss Jane to J. M. Tibbs 10-16-1869 (10-17-1869)
Ragan, Martha E. to William C. McBride 6-5-1866 (6-9-1866)
Ragen, Mary E. to T. B. Chester 1-11-1869
Rail, Jane to P. H. Hamilton 5-29-1865
Rainey, Ann to Edward Tidwell 6-23-1858
Rains, Christiana to M. B. Mitchell 8-20-1864 (8-21-1864)
Rains, Julia A. to A. T. P. Pool 1-4-1863 (1-7-1863)

Rains, Mary W. to S. W. Cox 12-18-1860 (12-20-1860)
Ray, Harriett B. to J. B. Craigh 7-15-1868
Reaves, Mary to J. B. Dodson 1-7-1860 (1-8-1860)
Redden, E. J. to Jno. H. Work 11-21-1861 (11-24-1861)
Redden, Palistrue to T. J. Work 2-1-1870 (2-3-1870)
Redden, S. E. to R. D. Steel 12-1-1866 (12-6-1866)
Redings, Malissa to William W. Stokey 4-27-1867 (4-28-1867)
Reed, A. C. L. to William M. Goforth 6-25-1867 (6-27-1867)
Reep, Louvina to John H. Derryberry 12-20-1869 (1-20-1870)
Reynolds, Mary E. to J. B. V. Shmittou 11-7-1866
Reynolds, Sophronia to John Albright 10-16-1858 (10-17-1858)
Rice, M. J. to J. W. Godfry 11-11-1863 (11-12-1863)
Richardson, Anna to George J. Estes 1-6-1869
Richardson, Lenora to H. C. Gentry 5-14-1870 (5-25-1870)
Richardson, M. H. to B. H. Johnson 12-6-1864 (not certified)
Richardson, Martha Ann to Thos. J. Harris 12-31-1868
Richardson, Mary to W. H. Taylor 1-16-1868
Richardson, P. L. to L. S. Russell 11-22-1858 (11-23-1858)
Richardson, Sarah to J. B. Adcock 8-23-1865 (8-24-1865)
Robertson, Eunice A. to John S. Ward 4-21-1859
Robertson, Mary A. to David Patterson 6-4-1870
Robertson, Mary M. to Wm. J. Dickson 10-11-1859
Roena, Paschall to Jos. Owen 7-30-1862
Rogers, E. to James Williams 10-27-1863
Rogers, Frances to T. D. Gunn? 2-2-1859 (2-3-1859)
Rooker, Amanda to Geo. W. Southerland 12-4-1860
Rooker, Rebecca P. to Harvey Page 10-22-1860 (10-28-1860)
Rose, Evaline to John Byers 2-16-1859
Rose, J. E. to Manuel Hatley 10-25-1865 (10-29-1865)
Ross, Cyntha J. to Kendrick Myatt 6-8-1866 (6-10-1866)
Ross, Susan M. to J. K. Porter 11-9-1865
Runnells, Geo. A. D. to Geo. W. Runnells 5-23-1862 (5-25-1862)
Runnells?, Fredonia A. to Ben F. Briant 12-26-1860
Russell, Charity to A. J. Petty 8-13-1859
Russell, M. C. to W. H. H. Laurence 7-1-1865 (7-2-1865)
Russell, M. E. to J. D. Boaze 8-18-1864 (8-25-1864)
Russell, Rebecca to Aquilla Tidwell 12-14-1859 (12-15-1859)
Rutlage, Eliza J. to Joel Williams 11-25-1869
Rye, Martha E. to Thos. C. Morris 11-28-1858
Sanders, Emily to E. B. Goodrich 11-5-1869 (11-14-1869)
Sanders, Parmelia to James Steel 2-14-1867
Satterfield, Sarah J. to Oscar Vanwanner no date (with Mar 1866)
Schmittou, Alsey Ann V. to John M. Potts 5-7-1870 (5-17-1870)
Schmittou, M. M. V. to J. W. Michel 10-17-1866
Schmittou, Marthy N. V. to J. R. Mitchel 2-5-1867 (2-6-1867)
Schmittou, Mary E. O. (V.?) to James F. Potts 1-7-1857 (1-8-1857)
Schmittou, Sophrona V. to Thos. W. McMurrey 5-3-1860
Scott, E. A. to J. N. Smith 10-3-1864 (10-6-1864)
Seals, Elizabeth to Geo. W. Seels 2-1-1862
Sears, Hulda C. to William E. Pendergrass 5-4-1867

Sears, Rebecca to John Sears 1-21-1865 (1-22-1865)
Self, Mary S. to J. N. Morrison 2-16-1869 (2-17-1869)
Self, Tabitha J. to John Frank Foster 12-17-1858
Sellars, Elizabeth to Jonah (Josiah?) Tidwell 2-11-1862 (2-12-1862)
Sellars, Margarett to Richard M. McGeehee 12-16-1868 (12-20-1868)
Sellars, Martha to Lindon A. Nalls 1-3-1859
Sellars, Sarah to Benjamin Prichard 3-23-1870 (3-24-1870)
Sellers, Almarinda to Jacob Beard 11-12-1864 (11-16-1864)
Sensing, Lydia J. to W. B. Batson 10-6-1857 (10-8-1857)
Sensing, Martha E. to John Forsythe 7-4-1867
Sensing, Mary E. to Jerry Forsythe 9-20-1866 (9-30-1866)
Sensing, Polly W. to J. W. Deen 5-2-1861
Sensing, Rebecca A. to William J. Ford 10-22-1866 (10-23-1866)
Sewell, Nancy to James Meek 7-5-1858
Shadic, Sophronia to Asa Bishop 4-8-1864 (4-10-1864)
Shelton, Catharine E. A. to Zachree Payne 9-3-1867 (9-5-1867)
Shelton, E. E. to W. C. Crunk 7-23-1869
Shelton, K. P. to R. P. Smith 2-20-1866
Shelton, L. W. to L. W. Damell 9-18-1863
Shelton, Lenora to Jas. M. Skelton 2-14-1865 (2-15-1865)
Shelton, M. G. to John T. Beck 11-2-1858 (11-3-1858)
Shelton, Martha to Daniel Moore 12-29-1857 (12-30-1857)
Shelton, Mary E. to Jno. M. Collin 1-1-1859 (1-2-1859)
Shelton, Nancy W. to Wm. Davidson 12-23-1857 (12-24-1857)
Shelton, Nelly to T. J. Ladd 1-18-1870 (1-19-1870)
Shelton, Sophia to Joseph A. Work 5-26-1868
Shivers?, Harriet M. to B. F. Walker 12-11-1858 (12-12-1858)
Simmons, Mary E. to Thomas Blackwell 8-23-1868
Simmons, Nancy E. to Wiley J. Baker 2-26-1868 (3-1-1868)
Simmons?, Lydia to D. D. Turner 7-20-1863 (7-24-1863)
Sims, Martha L. to Leroy D. Pack 10-3-1859 (10-5-1859)
Sims?, S. B. to S. J. Garland 6-23-1865 (6-25-1865)
Singleton, F. E. to W. L. Lewis 9-16-1870 (9-8?-1870)
Singleton, M. E. to John L. Reynolds 12-29-1870
Sinks, Bettie to Edward Adams 1-24-1864
Sinks?, Elizabeth A. to Sylvester Parker 9-29-1859
Sitton, S. E. to C. N. Colter 5-5-1864
Sizemore, Mary A. to J. L. Hatcher 2-9-1857 (2-12-1857)
Skelton, L. M. to W. V. Turner 8-4-1864
Slayden, E. F. to A. V. Geurin (Guinn?) 12-26-1865 (12-28-1865)
Slayden, Jane to J. J. Pickett 1-12-1861 (1-13-1861)
Slayden, Letsy to Burrel Hunter 3-28-1870
Slayden, Martha J. to Geo. K. Bone 1-19-1864 (1-20-1864)
Slayden, R. E. to William B. Bone 10-8-1870 (10-11-1870)
Slayden, S. P. to James C. Hunt 11-17-1858
Smith, Ann J. to J. M. McClelland 12-22-1858 (12-23-1858)
Smith, Eliza Jane to R. E. Fletcher 9-13-1859 (9-14-1859)
Smith, Elizabeth to L. J. Pack 2-11-1860 (2-2?-1860)
Smith, L. D. to J. M. Fielder 7-27-1870
Smith, N. J. to J. D. Hill 8-15-1863 (8-17-1863)

Southerland, A. A. to W. M. Brown 12-22-1860 (12-23-1860)
Southerland, Martha to Dennis Hudson 9-7-1861 (9-8-1861)
Sowells, Celia to Hyram Spencer 2-5-1857
Spears, Anna to George W. Luther 8-10-1867 (8-11-1867)
Speight, Dilly to St Clair Scott 10-28-1859 (2-18-1861)
Speight, Panie? to Jesse Hooper 2-24-1862 (2-27-1862)
Spencer, Indiana to W. C. Marsh 2-26-1861 (2-28-1861)
Spencer, Lathersy? to John Caselman 1-12-1867 (1-13-1867)
Spencer, Martha J. to H. A. Parker 12-29-1869 (12-30-1869)
Spencer, Susan to Jas. Sears 7-6-1864 (7-7-1864)
Spicer, Clarisa to J. M. Stuart 12-27-1865
Spicer, Tabitha to Richard Daniel 12-26-1867
Spradlin, E. E. to Houston Davis 4-2-1859
Spradling, Martha C. to John A. Smith 9-3-1868
Springer, Cary Jane to John D. Sugg 4-3-1857 (4-7-1857)
Springger, Sarah to J. M. Brazel 8-27-1866 (8-28-1866)
Stanfill, Victoria S. to Jas. J. Fentress 4-29-1865
Stark, Mary M. to J. C. Schmittou 9-17-1868 (9-20-1868)
Steeley, Mary to Wiley H. Bateman 6-15-1870 (6-16-1870)
Stewart, Nancy to James Mathis 8-28-1857 (8-29-1857)
Stinnett, C. T. to John A. Petty 7-31-1863
Stoke, L. T. to Wm. R. Deason 8-27-1864
Stokes, E. E. to W. C. Dean 11-24-1859
Stokes, Martha J. to Montgomery Jordon 12-28-1867 (12-29-1867)
Story, Elanora to W. J. W. Bateman 4-14-1864
Story, Mary to Geo. Latour 8-7-1864 (8-8-1864)
Streat, Nancy C. to J. W. Dotson 6-30-1858 (7-1-1858)
Street, Alcey A. to Abner Robinson 1-3-1860 (1-11-1860)
Street, Alice J. to W. S. Porch 8-21-1861 (9-4-1861)
Street, Elizer F. to H. W. Street 8-26-1867 (12-27-1867)
Street, M. F. to G. A. Williams 9-28-1863 (9-29-1863)
Street, Mary M. to James R. Williams 9-8-1858 (no return)
Street, Susan A. E. to Henry E. Pickett 6-1-1859 (6-2-1859)
Street?, Mary S. to Tho. J. Handlin 5-21-1859 (5-22-1859)
Stringfellow, M. A. to W. E. Higgins 8-12-1870 (8-14-1870)
Stroud, Atalanta V. to William E. Williams 3-17-1869 (3-18-1869)
Stuart, E. C. to A. H. Bell 4-2-1862 (4-9-1862)
Stuart, Mary A. to Charles A. Bradley 5-24-1860 (5-26-1860)
Stuart, Mary J. to James M. Brown 12-24-1866 (12-7?-1866)
Stuart, Nancy C. to R. P. Jackson 6-30-1857 (7-1-1857)
Sugg, Elizabeth to John W. Easley 3-12-1857
Sugg, Mary C. to William M. Petty 9-23-1868 (9-25-1868)
Sugg, Sarah M. to Wiley M. Russell 12-9-1867
Sulivan, Sarena C. to William G. Lampley 11-14-1868 (11-24-1868)
Sullivan, Martha to F. M. Tidwell 11-3-1857
Sutherland, Mary to A. P. Brown 10-27-1869
Sutherland, Narcissy R. to W. M. Dorrin (Dunn?) 3-31-1870
Sutherland, Sarah J. to Simpson H. Hooper 1-1-1866
Sweaney, E.J. to W. J. Shelton 8-12-1870 (8-14-1870)
Swift, E. F. to Saml. H. Adkins 9-2-1864 (9-15-1864)

Swinney, Mary J. to W. B. Joslin 7-10-1869 (7-11-1869)
Tally, Sarah M. to Lavell H. Hooper 9-22-1860 (9-23-1860)
Tate, Amanda to Edmond M. Tidwell 2-24-1859
Tate, Artela to T. J. Anglin 1-17-1866
Tate, Artela to James H. Yates 1-8-1870
Tate, Elizabeth to F. M. Cathey 1-16-1861 (1-17-1861)
Tatom, Amanda to John Rogers 12-28-1870 (12-29-1870)
Tatom, Jane to Henderson Brazzle 12-28-1867 (12-29-1867)
Tatom, Lotty to S. J. A. Wills 1-31-1865 (2-5-1865)
Tatom, Sarah to Thomas Whitlock 11-5-1866 (11-7-1866)
Tatom, Susan to Reuben Manley 4-19-1858
Taylor, Ann to W. H. Vale 2-2-1859
Taylor, Dilly Ann to J. B. Bull 3-2-1866 (3-8-1866)
Taylor, Elizabeth to Fountain Jones 8-9-1869 (8-11-1869)
Taylor, Henrietta to J. T. Mitchell 7-3-1870
Taylor, Letticia to R. M. Gillmore 4-29-1864
Taylor, Louisa to G. W. Smith 11-7-1857 (11-8-1857)
Taylor, Sarah to Joseph Hall 10-12-1860 (10-14-1860)
Terrel, M. J. to C. Finney 6-7-1864 (6-9-1864)
Thomas, Elizer to Joshua G. Estes 8-31-1868 (9-3-1868)
Thomison, Margarett to C. L. Hase 12-11-1865
Thompson, Adeline E. to Alfred S. Capps 9-8-1862 (9-10-1862)
Thompson, Docia to Lewis Larkins 12-7-1867
Thompson, Dolly J. to W. J. Norris 10-14-1865
Thompson, Emily J. to Jeremiah Thompson 4-5-1859
Thompson, Jenny to William Lewis 9-24-1869 (9-26-1869)
Thompson, Latitia Bella to Gustin Hatley 1-10-1869
Thompson, Ludeena to W. G. Carter 6-17-1857
Thompson, Mary to Wm. Vanhook 11-25-1861
Thompson, Mary D. to B. F. Larkins 11-10-1869
Thompson, Missouri E. to Joab L. Shelton 2-11-1867
Thompson, Sarah A. to Joseph H. Hendrick 12-31-1859
Thompson, Susan A. to Thomas Taylor 11-10-1869
Thompson, Susan V. to John Brim 8-30-1870 (9-1-1870)
Thompson, Tennessee A. to Batty Richardson 10-8-1870 (10-9-1870)
Thompson, W. A. to F. Capeheart 5-17-1864 (5-19-1864)
Thornton?, H. P. to W. M. Green 11-30-1858 (12-1-1858)
Tidwell, Amanda to M. L. Gentry 4-23-1870 (4-24-1870)
Tidwell, Anna to Robt. Walker 11-13-1860 (11-22-1860)
Tidwell, Bedy E. to J. T. Johnston 1-27-1866 (1-28-1866)
Tidwell, Eliza J. to John F. Cunningham 9-18-1865 (9-19-1865)
Tidwell, Eliza J. to David H. Rice 5-21-1861
Tidwell, Mahala to M. W. Clifton 10-26-1859 (10-27-1859)
Tidwell, Margaret to M. V. Anglin 8-27-1864
Tidwell, Mary M. to John Farhan 8-5-1861 (8-8-1861)
Tidwell, Penny? to Jos. Sullivan 1-19-1860 (1-22-1860)
Tidwell, Rachel to Abner Dunnagan 2-28-1865
Tidwell, Sarah J. to Andrew J. Sullivan 7-14-1870 (7-17-1870)
Tidwell, Sophrona to J. W. Anglin 4-1-1859
Tidwell, Susan to W. M. Hogins 7-12-1866

Timmons, Martha to Stephen Bagwell 6-4-1863 (6-5-1863)
Tingler, Letty to Thomas Booker 5-2-1870 (5-8-1870)
Tolar, E. J. to Leroy Heath 3-20-1860 (3-21-1860)
Toler, Myrom? to James M. Gilbert 11-25-1867
Tomlinson, H. C. to Wm. M. Green 8-9-1864 (8-11-1864)
Truby, Clara E. to Thos. J. Anderson 5-15-1869 (5-18-1869)
Tucker, Elizabeth to Wm. D. Hughes 9-16-1870
Turner, Agnes M. to Allen Anchor 2-28-1870 (3-3-1870)
Turner, Elvira to Tho. Baker 11-7-1860
Turner, Frances to W. W. Adams 9-25-1864
Turnidge, Mary to John S. Sanders 1-22-1864 (1-24-1864)
Underhill, Elizabeth to John H. Tidwell 10-17-1859
Underwood, Jane C. to Wm. Clymer? 2-21-1861 (2-23-1861)
Underwood, Margaret to Charley Climer 3-10-1858
Underwood, Martha to Riley Bradford 8-11-1860 (8-12-1860)
Vales, Sarah E. to John Nicks 4-4-1859 (4-22-1859)
Vanhook, India A. to D. G. Smith 4-5-1869 (4-11-1869)
Vanhook, M. M. to W. C. Averett 6-17-1858 (6-18-1858)
Vanhook, Susan A. E. to Jacob Chesman 3-13-1858 (3-14-1858)
Varden, Catharine to Orvel Garland 1-7-1867
Vineyard, Adeline to Tho. D. Petty 10-27-1858 (10-31-1858)
Vineyard, R. J. to W. S. Brown 4-1-1861 (4-14-1861)
Walch, Martha L. to A. J. McClure 2-28-1861
Walker, Anna to George Clardy 11-20-1865 (11-21-1865)
Walker, M. M. to W. C. Tubb 1-21-1863
Walker, Margarett to Thomas B. Sanders 12-31-1868
Walker, Martha W. to J. L. Talley 9-27-1865
Walker, Matilda J. to Wm. S. Crowell 1-26-1859 (1-27-1859)
Walker, N. M. to E. J. Dawson 12-23-1869
Walker, Ritha S. to Alexander Woollund 12-27-1862 (12-28-1862)
Walker, S. M. to Wiley B. Deen 9-22-1870
Walker, Tennessee J. to John M. Hudson 2-7-1865
Wall, Mary E. to Thomas O. Prockter 8-2-1869 (8-6-1869)
Waller, Rebecca to Samuel H. Story 7-22-1869
Ward, R. V. to M. R. Cloud? 10-6-1860
Warden, Sarah to James Patterson 12-3-1866 (12-4-1866)
Warner, Elizabeth to Danl. Bullard 2-19-1862 (2-20-1862)
Washburn, Mary E. to James H. Crim 12-14-1868 (12-15-1868)
Watley, H. T. to H. H. Harris 4-11-1861
Waynick, Ann to Lee Bradford 10-22-1870
Waynick, Eliza J. to M. V. Patterson 6-8-1861 (6-9-1861)
Waynick, L. E. to Ellas Brewer 6-25-1870 (6-26-1870)
Waynick, Mary E. to Benjamin S. Adams 12-14-1866
Waynick, Mary E. to John C. Adams 6-10-1860
Weakley, E. H. to Thos. Stark 5-6-1864
Weakley, Mary E. to P. C. Freeman 4-15-1863 (4-16-1863)
Weems, Martha J. to James F. Vance 12-26-1868 (12-27-1868)
Welch, E. to Jos. Hassum 12-24-1861 (12-25-1861)
Welker, Mary to W. R. Reynolds 6-4-1866 (6-7-1866)
West, E. to T. Hargroves 7-25-1859

White, Calledonia to William M. Hutchison 11-16-1868 (11-19-1868)
White, Eliza to Wm. Buttery 1-26-1857 (1-2?-1857)
White, Lorena to W. C. Reed 12-26-1866 (12-28-1866)
Whitfield, M. E. to W. B. Joslin 7-12-1864 (7-15-1864)
Whitfield, Martha to Lenno Pack 11-9-1869 (11-14-1869)
Whitfield, Mary Ann to James Lewis 1-19-1867
Whitlock, Maranda to E. L. Bowen 1-9-1864 (1-10-1864)
Whitlock, Mary to Egbert Work 6-30-1868 (7-?-1868)
Wilkes, Elizabeth to James H. Morris 3-14-1870 (3-17-1870)
Wilkins, Sarah J. to Saml. H. Evans 9-13-1858 (9-14-1858)
Willey, Geo. Ann to Wm. Austin 9-18-1858 (9-19-1858)
Willey, Malissa to W. T. Waller 10-4-1862 (10-5-1862)
Willey, Nancy L. to James M. Walker 7-15-1869
Willey, Rody A. to George Hallaburton 2-13-1866
Williams, A. F. to C. Hickerson 8-18-1866 (8-19-1866)
Williams, Ann to W. J. McClelland 3-27-1860
Williams, E. to S. Adams 11-27-1862
Williams, E. E. to A. C. Henley 4-5-1862 (4-6-1862)
Williams, Ellen M. to Jesse B. Speight 9-28-1868 (9-29-1868)
Williams, Frances to S. E. Choat 12-20-1866
Williams, Nancy E. to William T. Bledsoe 3-26-1868
Williams, Sarah J. to Thos. L. Justice 5-29-1860 (5-31-1860)
Williams, Susan to Wm. Carrall 8-15-1861
Winfrey, Ann to Thomas Nicholas 3-2-1866 (3-5-1866)
Wood, Elizabeth to James A. Morgan 8-10-1865
Wooddy, America to Thos. Anfienson 7-23-1864
Woods, Louisa to W. L. Murphy 9-7-1870
Woodward, E. C. to Henry C. Callen 8-25-1857
Woodward, Elizabeth to James M. Linzy 2-2-1867 (2-3-1867)
Woodward, Lucy R. to Robert P. Williams 2-12-1870 (2-13-1870)
Woody, Sarah E. to John A. Springer 9-1-1868
Work, Sarah Ann to J. W. J. Shelton 12-6-1869 (12-9?-1869)
Wright, E. J. to Thos. J. Hooper 10-6-1860 (10-7-1860)
Wright, Rebecca Ann to W. M. Hirt 11-7-1866 (1-20-1867)
Yates, Ann to A. Marsh 11-12-1860 (11-29-1860)
Yates, Martha E. to William T. Thompson 9-2-1868
Yates, Rebecca P. to James W. Nall 11-6-1865
Yeats, E. L. to Thos. J. Isbell 7-28-1870 (7-29-1870)
Zodake, Florence to Edward T. Jones 11-1-1870
_____, H. O. to W. A. Pendergrass 3-14-1863
_____, _____ to Cane J. Marsh 4-7-1869 (4-8-1869)

www.ingramcontent.com/pod-product-compliance
Lightning Source LLC
Chambersburg PA
CBHW081926170426
43200CB00014B/2848